# Day by Day

# Day by Day

*180 Days of Hope and Encouragement*

## Zac Bauermaster

ConnectEDD Publishing

Hanover, Pennsylvania

This publication is available at discount pricing when purchased in quantity for educational purposes, promotions, or fundraisers. For inquiries and details, contact the publisher at: info@connecteddpublishing.com

Published by ConnectEDD Publishing LLC
Hanover, PA
www.connecteddpublishing.com

Cover Design: Kheila Casas

Day by Day —1st ed. Paperback
ISBN    979-8-9988361-5-2

# Praise for *Day by Day*

*Day by Day* is exactly what so many of us need—a gentle, grace-filled reminder that God is near in every moment. Zac Bauermaster writes with honesty and heart, offering encouragement that's both practical and deeply spiritual. These daily reflections help quiet the noise of life so you can hear God's voice more clearly. I'm grateful for Zac's faithfulness to point people back to the hope we have in Jesus—one day at a time.

    –Tasha Layton | Singer, Songwriter, and Author of *Look What You've Done*

With each hope-filled reflection, *Day by Day* is like a morning high-five from Heaven—a reminder that God sees you, loves you, and is cheering for you. Zac is love in action and turns simple moments into sacred encouragement.

    –Jody Luke | President, Love Does

Zac Bauermaster's devotional will spur you on to love and good deeds! It is an encouraging and challenging call to embrace each day as an opportunity to grow closer to Christ and look beyond ourselves. This book is a gift for anyone seeking to live with purpose and hope, rooted in the timeless truth of Scripture.

    –Peter Greer | President & CEO, Hope International

Dr. Zac Bauermaster's passion for making a meaningful impact is both evident and inspiring. While I'm impressed by all he's accomplished at an early age and the influence he's earned, what stands out even more is his deep commitment to helping others grow—spiritually, personally, and professionally. That heart for others shines through in these pages. In a world that often moves too fast, this book offers readers a much-needed invitation to pause, reflect, and return to what matters most: loving God and one another. It's a refreshing call back to the basics—and a powerful reminder that transformation doesn't happen all at once, but day by day.

–Ed Herr | Executive Chairman, Herr's Foods

This book points us back to the truth: that there is hope for the hopeless, encouragement for the discouraged, and rest for the weary. Zac's relatable stories intertwined with practical wisdom remind us to always set our minds on things above. A clear, positive read!

–Hannah Crews | Author, Speaker, Social Media Personality, @hannahcrews.blog

In a world full of hurry, this devotional invites you to slow down and build a rhythm that actually sustains your soul. *Day by Day* isn't about checking a box—it's about anchoring your heart in Scripture, honesty, and hope. Zac Bauermaster has created more than a devotional—he's given us a daily companion to walk closer with God and live more intentionally. A must-read for anyone seeking faith that's lived, not just learned.

–Dr. Brad Johnson | Author, Speaker, and Educator

Zac Bauermaster's writing is a breath of fresh air—rooted in real life, overflowing with hope, and always pointing readers back to what matters most. His gift is making faith practical, accessible, and deeply encouraging, whether you're facing a mountain or just another Monday. I'm grateful for Zac's voice in our community and for the way he lives out the love he writes about, day by day.

–Fred McNaughton | President, WJTL, Station Manager, and Radio Host

*Day by Day* is a breath of fresh air for those navigating the demands of daily life. Zac writes with authenticity and grace, reminding us that hope isn't found in hustle but in walking with Jesus—one day, one moment at a time. These short devotions meet you where you are and gently point you back to who God is. I'll be keeping this on my desk—and in my heart—for the days I need to refocus on what truly matters.

–Jessica Cabeen | Speaker, Author, Principal, Blogger for Christian Educators

I've watched Zac grow from a young boy into a man who leads with quiet strength and deep faith. *Day by Day* is a beautiful reflection of the way he lives his life—grounded in God's Word, intentional in every moment, and committed to encouraging others. This devotional isn't just a book; it's an overflow of a life surrendered to Christ. I believe it will bless anyone who reads it, just as Zac's life and leadership have blessed so many already.

–Jeff Rutt | CEO, Keystone Custom Homes, Chairman/Founder, HOPE International

Once again, Zac has outdone himself with a book that is so needed in today's world. In *Day by Day*, Zac not only challenges us to spend time in the Word and draw closer to God, but also provides a blueprint for doing so. Each day's entry invites you into Scripture, prompts meaningful reflection, and helps you deepen your roots that last far beyond the 180 days. With heartfelt honesty and biblical depth, Zac has created a devotional that not only inspires you but also equips you for whatever season of life you are in. This is the kind of book you'll come back to again and again.

–Dr. Tyler Cook | Principal, Speaker, Author

If you're looking for the simple yet profound truths about who God is, who He has made you to be, and to center your life around Christ every day, read *Day by Day*. Zac Bauermaster is a gifted, down-to-earth writer who is full of gospel truths, captivating stories, and encouragement for your soul. So many life lessons that can take years to learn are shared right here in this book from his heart to yours; soak them in!

–Jenna Dombach | Executive Assistant at The Leaders of Faith Foundation (and Zac's former student and basketball player)

Dr. Zac Bauermaster beautifully blends real-life stories with biblical truth, encouraging a daily habit of prayer and reflection. Each entry invites you to pause, refocus, and grow closer to God in a simple, relatable way. In today's fast-paced world, it's the perfect tool for anyone seeking to build a stronger, more intentional faith, one day at a time.

–Katie Wood | Author, Speaker, Thought Leader

Are you a people-pleaser, a worrier, or one who asks, "What now, God?" or "Why, God?" Whatever description fits you, Zac has penned 180 devotional thoughts and journaling prompts that allow us to pause, take a moment, and realign our walk with our Savior and his love for us. The preface alone bears daily reading and meditation. God created you with a purpose: live for Him!

–Dr. Jonathan Roux | Professor of Education at Martin Luther College, New Ulm, MN.

In *Day by Day*, Zac Bauermaster reminds us that faith doesn't require mountaintop experiences or long pilgrimages—it can be found right where we are: at the kitchen table, in the carpool line, or in a quiet moment first thing in the morning or right before bed. This devotional offers a personal, accessible, and intentional way to draw near to God—one day at a time. Whether you're just beginning your faith journey or have walked with Jesus for years, *Day by Day* creates space to pause, reflect, and be encouraged.

–Steve Dang | Chief Ministry Officer, Senior Vice President, Valley Christian Schools, San Jose, CA.

*Day by Day* is like a deep breath for your soul! With every page, Zac gently reminds you that you don't have to hustle your way through life—you just need to keep showing up and walking with Jesus. This book is for you if your heart craves peace, your calendar is packed, and you need a daily dose of grace and truth. Whether you're a teacher, parent, or just feeling stretched thin, this devotional will help you slow down, refocus, and remember what really matters.

–Kayla Dornfeld, 2019 North Dakota Teacher of the Year, 2020 Top USA Educator of the Year, CEO, Top Dog Teaching Inc.

# Dedication

To my wife, Carly—
I can't write a book without dedicating it to you
because I couldn't do it without you.

To my kids, Olivia, Eliot, and Isaac—
Follow Jesus day by day.

To my pastor and friend, Michael Brown—
Your life and leadership consistently point me to Jesus, day by day.

# Table of Contents

# Preface

Pause and take a deep breath. Life moves fast. Life is hard. Between the demands of work, family, church, and everything in between, it's easy to drift into survival mode—living for the next deadline, the next accomplishment, the next item on the calendar, the next moment of rest, or the next vacation. But deep down, we know we were made for more than just making it through the day. We were created to live with purpose, to grow in grace, and to reflect God's goodness in our everyday lives.

This devotional was created to help us take life day by day—to slow down and pay attention to our time, our hearts, our habits, and our walk with God—in a way that draws us closer to the One who gave us this life in the first place. The One who is sovereign above all—who holds the universe in His hands and still cares intimately about the details of our lives. The One who has written every page of our stories, who knew us before we took our first breath, and lovingly ordained each of our steps before we came to be. The One who works all things together for our good and His glory. The Alpha and the Omega, the beginning and the end, whose goodness never fails and whose presence never leaves. This devotional is not just about slowing down—it's about drawing near to Him.

At its core, this devotional is about the heart. Everything we do overflows from the heart. There's no better place to go for heart transformation than the Word of God. There are a lot of self-help books, podcasts, and articles filled with tips and tricks—but nothing transforms like the Word. Scripture doesn't just *inform us*; it *transforms us*—softening and shaping our hearts. And that's exactly what we need—not just better routines, but renewed hearts. Through the grace of God and His Word, we can find the true hope that transcends circumstances—hope that never fades and encouragement that comes from our Living Hope, Jesus Christ. Too often, we look for hope in things of this world, which only leave us empty, unfulfilled, and wanting more. But the hope we have in Christ is living and everlasting—it fills us with peace, purpose, and joy that the world cannot offer.

Across these devotions, you'll notice recurring themes: being in the Word of God, meditating on it deeply, walking in humility, surrendering control, praying continually, practicing solitude. and staying connected in community with others. Many of these themes will be repeated throughout—on purpose. I know I need the daily reminders, and I need the daily reminders to keep coming back.

You'll be encouraged to live intentionally, to steward your time and gifts well, and to remember that you are not meant to do life alone. The truth is, it's easy to look back with regret. It's just as easy to look ahead with worry. But the life we're called to live is built day by day—in small, faithful steps, right where we are. And in those steps, we can trust that God provides exactly what we need for today—our daily bread—sustaining us with His grace, strength, and presence moment by moment.

My hope is that these short devotionals offer clarity in the chaos and strength for the journey. Whether you read one in the quiet of the morning, during the day, or right before your head hits the pillow, I pray each entry helps you live a little more fully, love a little more deeply, and walk a little more closely with the One who says, "Well done, good and faithful servant."

This devotional is about real, everyday life—lived in light of eternity. One step at a time. Day by day.

# How Each Day Works

Each day in this devotional is designed to help you slow down and draw near to God by following Jesus—not out of routine, but out of relationship. Life moves fast, and it's easy to fall into hurried mode moving from one thing to the next. But when we pause to be still before God, we begin to build rhythms that not only sustain us, but strengthen us for our good and, ultimately, His glory.

This devotional was created to help you cultivate habits of grace and spiritual disciplines long after the 180 days are over—reading God's Word, meditating on it through reflection and journaling, turning your heart to Him in prayer, solitude, and walking in community with others who are doing the same. These are the rhythms that shape a deeper faith in Jesus—day by day.

These practices are not passive; they require perseverance and intentionality. Just as we wouldn't expect to grow physically healthy without effort, we can't expect to grow spiritually mature without discipline. We don't practice these habits to earn God's love, but to grow in it. They take effort, not to impress Him, but to know Him more deeply. They are rhythms of grace that draw us closer to the heart of Jesus and anchor us in His truth—day by day. And as His Word takes root in us, it begins to overflow from us—shaping not just how we think, but how we live. We become not just listeners of the Word, but doers, living out our faith in everyday moments. Here's what each daily devotion includes:

**Short Title:** A word or phrase to center your focus for the day—something that captures the heart of the devotion.

**Verse of the Day:** A key verse that anchors the devotion. While this single verse offers a starting point, you're encouraged to go back and read the full passage to understand the broader context. God's Word is best read as a whole, not in pieces—and truth becomes clearer when seen in the light of Scripture's full story. As Donald Whitney (2014) wisely put it, "No spiritual discipline is more important than the intake of God's Word. Nothing can substitute for it. There simply is no healthy Christian life apart from a diet of the milk and meat of Scripture." Let the daily verse lead you deeper into God's living Word.

**Devotion:** A short, honest reflection rooted in real life. Some days you'll laugh. Some days you might cry. But every day, you'll be pointed back to the truth of God's Word and His faithfulness in the everyday moments. These devotions aren't polished sermons—they're real, grace-filled reminders that God is with you in the mess and the mundane.

**Journal:** A question or reflection to help us engage more deeply. Don't just think about it—write it down. Journaling is a form of meditation and makes space for God to speak personally. Thomas Watson (1981) said, "The reason we come away so cold from reading the Word is because we do not warm ourselves by the fire of meditation." When I say meditation, I'm not referring to emptying our minds, but instead, filling our minds with Scripture. It's a way to process, pray, and grow. Even a few scribbled thoughts can open the door for clarity and conviction. Over time, journaling becomes a powerful way to look back and see how God has been working in and through our hearts—shaping, refining, and drawing us closer to Him, day by day. Don't worry about writing the perfect journal entry—there's no such thing. Just pour out your heart, and let God meet you where you are.

**One-Sentence Prayer:** A short prayer to help you turn everything over to God. It's simple, yet purposeful—meant to be carried with you and repeated throughout your day. When you're feeling stretched, distracted, overwhelmed, or simply want to praise God, let this prayer re-center your heart. Let this one-sentence prayer fill your mind all day and lead to more prayer. As David Mathis (2016) says in his book *Habits of Grace*, "You have God's ear. Don't waste it." After listening to God through His Word and meditating on His Word, speak to God through prayer.

**Further hope and encouragement**: Each day concludes with a suggested reading—usually the full chapter of the verse or an additional section of Scripture. This is where the depth happens. Don't skip it.

Let God's Word continue to speak, challenge, and encourage you beyond the devotional itself. There is always more to the story—more grace, more truth, more of Him.

This devotion isn't about checking a box. It's about becoming someone who walks with Jesus. So open the Word. Reflect honestly. Write boldly. Pray consistently. Stay connected in community. God is softening and shaping your heart to become more like Jesus–day by day.

# One Page at a Time

*All the days ordained for me were written in your book*
*before one of them came to be.*
*Psalm 139:16*

You have a purpose. God has placed you exactly where you're supposed to be, doing exactly what you're supposed to do, at exactly the right time. Maybe it's not what you thought you'd be doing or where you hope to be in five years, but today, it's where you are. If you're like me, it's easy to spend too much time dwelling on the past or worrying about the future. Life often pulls our focus to what has been or what might be, but God invites us to be present in the moments He's given us. Every person, every conversation, and every interaction is part of His perfect plan for our lives. We don't want to miss the people, moments, and opportunities right in front of us.

As David says in Psalm 139, "All the days ordained for me were written in your book before one of them came to be" (v.16). Your life is a book written by Almighty God. You're on the exact page you're supposed to be. Maybe something is bothering you from the past, and you want to flip back a few pages. You may be worried about the future and want to flip ahead a few pages to see what will happen. Instead, trust God to equip you for everything He's called you to do today. God wrote your story before you were born, and He knows every detail. You're on the page you're meant to be on—take it one page at a time.

**Journal:** How often do you find yourself looking back or worrying about the future? Reflect on today's verse, Psalm 139:16. How can you focus more on the "page" you are on right now, trusting that God has a purpose for you in this moment? Write about how you can embrace the present and the opportunities it holds, even if they don't align with your previous expectations or future plans.

**One-sentence prayer:** Heavenly Father, You have me exactly where I'm supposed to be, doing exactly what I'm supposed to do, at exactly the right time.

***Further hope and encouragement: Psalm 139***

## DAY 2

# Cast All Your Anxiety

*Cast all your anxiety on him because he cares for you.*
1 Peter 5:7

Ilove fishing with my son. When he started baiting his own hook and removing his fish, it became even more enjoyable. Don't tell anyone, but I use a glove when I take the fish off the hook. While teaching Isaac to fish at a friend's pond, I showed him how to open the bail, hold the line with his finger, pull the rod back, and cast as far into the pond as possible. Some days, fishing goes smoothly—we catch plenty of fish, and the lines stay untangled. Other days? It seems like the only thing I do is spend my time untangling my son's fishing line. But here's what I've taught him: "When your line gets tangled, don't try to untangle it yourself. Call me over and hand your rod to me right away." Why? When he tries to untangle the line himself, it only makes things worse.

We often carry the weight of anxiety like a tangled fishing line. The pressures of daily life—relationships, responsibilities, and the demands on our time—can feel overwhelming. But imagine ourselves fishing, with each cast being an intentional effort to throw our anxieties far from us. Now, picture Jesus standing in the water, waiting for us to cast those burdens on Him. Here's the catch: if we don't release the line, it stays with us, turning into a tangled mess. The same is true for anxiety. When we cling to it or try to manage it ourselves, the knots tighten and the lines tangle. But when we let go and trust Jesus to take it, we experience the peace only He can provide. Today, let's name our anxieties one by one. Let's visualize putting each one on the hook and casting them to Jesus. If the lines get tangled, let's not try to untangle them ourselves—let's hand the rod over to Jesus. He cares deeply for us and is ready to take our burdens. Remember, life's challenges are lighter when we trust the One who leads us. Let's follow Jesus today.

**Journal:** What anxieties are weighing you down today? Are you trying to untangle the "line" yourself, only making things worse? How can you cast them to Jesus and trust Him to carry what you were never meant to hold?

**One-sentence prayer:** Heavenly Father, I cast all my anxiety on You today.

***Further hope and encouragement: 1 Peter 5:5-14***

## DAY 3

# The Heart

*But the Lord said to Samuel, "Do not consider his appearance or height,*
*for I have rejected him. The Lord does not look at the things man looks at.*
*Man looks at the outward appearance, but the Lord looks at the heart."*
1 Samuel 16:7

My grandfather, Pap-Pap, was a car salesman for fifty-four years and owned the Stoner-Wade Ford dealership in our hometown. He loved a clean car and you could often find him cleaning his car when it looked as if it didn't need to be cleaned at all. My first car was a green 1999 Ford Explorer Sport. On the days I had "Eddy" looking spotless (everyone needs to name their vehicle), I'd drive it to the top of the driveway so he could see it from the front window while watching *The Price is Right*. But on the days I didn't have it cleaned, I'd park it lower, hidden behind a tree so he wouldn't notice. One summer day, I spent hours washing and waxing it, determined to impress my grandfather. When I drove it up to his house, he came outside to inspect it. He looked over the shiny exterior, but then to my surprise, he walked over to the driver's side, opened the door, and as he did, an empty plastic water bottle fell to the ground. He looked up at me and said, "The outside looks great, but don't forget to take care of the inside."

That moment has stuck with me, reminding me that looking good on the outside means nothing if the inside is neglected. It's a lesson I've come to realize more and more in life. We often focus on outward appearances—on how things look to others—while neglecting what truly matters: our hearts. Saul, in the Bible, was a man who focused on outward appearance. Driven by insecurity and self-image, he sought to control others and win approval, but his heart was far from God. David, on the other hand, wasn't concerned with how he appeared to others. He spent his days caring for his flock, not for fame, but because of his deep love and obedience to God. God saw David's heart, not his outward qualifications, and chose him as king. Just like the lesson my Pap-Pap taught me, it's a reminder that taking care of what's on the inside is what truly matters. We may be tempted to focus on external success, but God calls us to tend to the condition of our hearts. So, today, "don't forget to take care of the inside."

**Journal:** Reflect on something you might be focusing on outwardly that is distracting you from taking care of your heart. What do you need to stop doing to focus more on what's inside?

**One-sentence prayer:** Heavenly Father, help me focus on nurturing my heart to align with Your will today.

*Further hope and encouragement: 1 Samuel 13, Proverbs 4:23*

# DAY 4
# Room In the Inn

*And she gave to her firstborn, a son. She wrapped him in cloths and placed*
*him in a manger, because there was no room for them in the inn.*
*Luke 2:7*

Like many stories in the Bible, this one both amazes and convicts me. When the time came for Jesus to be born, He was placed in a manger because there was no room for Him in the inn. What?! The Savior of the world—the King of kings, the Great I Am, the Rescuer, Yahweh—was about to be born, and the innkeeper essentially said, "I'm sorry, we're full tonight. There's no room for you." How could they not have room or at least make room for Him? Did they have any idea who they were turning away?

Then, I step back, and it hits me—I am more like the innkeeper than I'd like to admit. My days are packed with responsibilities: at school, at home, coaching, at church, and in the community. My schedule is full. And then there's Jesus, wanting to spend time with me every day. Without even realizing it, I respond like the innkeeper: "Sorry, Jesus, my day is full. I have so much going on. Maybe another morning or night this week." But that can't be! How about you? Reflect honestly—are you making room for Jesus in your life? If your life were a hotel, would the sign outside say "Vacancy" or "No Vacancy"? Do you find yourself saying, "Not today, Jesus, my plate is too full"? We must be intentional about making room for Him. There is nothing more important we could do with our time than spend it with Him. Don't be like the innkeeper—make room for Jesus.

**Journal:** What are the things in your life that tend to push Jesus out of your daily routine? How can you intentionally create space for Him?

**One-sentence prayer:** Heavenly Father, help me to clear the clutter from my life and make room for You every single day.

***Further hope and encouragement: Luke 2:1-6***

# DAY 5
# Be Like Jesus

*Your attitude should be the same as that of Christ Jesus.*
*Philippians 2:5*

I'm a big sports fan. I love basketball, and my favorite player of all time is Michael Jordan. I'm not here to debate whether Michael Jordan or LeBron James is the greatest because I already know—it's Michael Jordan. When a young Kobe Bryant moved to the United States from Italy, he fell in love with Michael Jordan's game and wanted to model his own play after him. Do you remember the Gatorade commercials with the song, "If I Could Be Like Mike"? A lot of kids wanted to be like him, but Kobe was different. He didn't just admire Michael—he studied him. He watched all of Jordan's games, analyzing how he dribbled, shot, and competed. He even waited outside the Chicago Bulls' locker room just to talk to him. Jordan's trainer once said, "Kobe looks at Michael Jordan as a reference book, an encyclopedia—whatever you want to call it. He didn't look at him as a fan. He wanted to absorb the knowledge that MJ had" (Grover, as cited in Botkin, 2020). And Kobe didn't just learn about Jordan—he put that knowledge into practice. He wanted to think like Michael, act like Michael, and play like Michael.

As followers of Christ, we must never stop learning, studying, and pursuing Jesus. Like Kobe's relentless pursuit to be like Jordan, we must be humble and teachable, always striving to grow more like Christ. Our goal isn't just to know about Jesus—it's to live like Him. Kobe didn't study Michael just to admire him; he studied him to embody his game. In the same way, let's not just be fans of Jesus. Let's spend time with Him, learn how He lived, how He spoke, and how He loved others—so we can reflect Him in our daily lives. Charles Spurgeon said, "Consider Jesus, often think of him, try to copy him" (Spurgeon, n.d.). The world doesn't need more people who just know about Jesus; it needs people who live like Jesus. So today, let's not just look up to Him—let's be like Him.

**Journal:** In what ways are you intentionally growing to be more like Jesus? What is one habit you can start today that will help you live more like Him?

**One-sentence prayer:** Heavenly Father, help me to not just know about You, but to truly live like You in my words, actions, and heart.

***Further hope and encouragement: Philippians 2***

# DAY 6
# Don't Lose Hope

*Have I not commanded you? Be strong and courageous.*
*Do not be terrified; do not be discouraged for the Lord your*
*God will be with you wherever you go.*
*Joshua 1:9*

Are you feeling discouraged today? Is life not going as you had hoped or planned? Are you tired of pushing forward, only to feel like you're standing still? Maybe the weight of responsibilities feels too heavy, or the daily grind has drained your energy. Do you find yourself stuck in a cycle of exhaustion, stress, or worry? Are you facing disappointments in your career, relationships, or personal goals? Does it feel like no matter how much effort you put in, the challenges just keep piling up? Are you losing sight of joy, weighed down by the struggles of today? Do your problems seem to be growing while your view of God is shrinking?

Pause and take a deep breath. No matter what you're facing, have faith and don't lose hope. God has commanded us to be strong and courageous, not because life is easy, but because He is with us wherever we go (Joshua 1:9). Even when life feels overwhelming, remember that God's strength is made perfect in our weakness. Paul Tripp (2014) describes biblical faith as examining reality but making God our meditation. If you're anything like me, here's the struggle: We often meditate on our problems, causing them to seem bigger and more insurmountable. Instead, we must look at our realities through the lens of God's greatness. When our view of God becomes smaller, our problems seem larger. But when our view of God becomes bigger, our problems shrink in comparison. God is greater than any hardship you face. By faith, turn to Him and hold onto hope today.

**Journal:** Reflect on a current challenge or discouragement you're facing. Has your perspective of the problem grown larger than your view of God? Take a moment to meditate on God's greatness and His promises. How can this shift in focus help you move forward with renewed strength and hope today?

**One-sentence prayer:** Heavenly Father, You are bigger than any problem or discouragement I face today.

**Further hope and encouragement: Joshua 1, Psalm 42**

## DAY 7

# Who Are You Working For?

*Whatever you do, work at it with all your heart,*
*as working for the Lord, not for men.*
*Colossians 3:23*

I don't know about you, but I tend to be a people-pleaser. I can get so caught up in seeking the approval of others that I lose sight of my true purpose. When my focus shifts to pleasing others, I fall short of fully embracing the life God has called me to live. Life isn't about meeting everyone else's expectations or pursuing personal gain. True living is about honoring God, reflecting His goodness, pursuing excellence with all our hearts, and maximizing the unique gifts He's entrusted to each of us for His glory. At its core, life is about humbly serving others and showing up every day with a commitment to give our best in all we do. It's about recognizing that everything we do reflects the One for whom we are ultimately living.

Colossians 3:23 reminds us, "Whatever you do, work at it with all your heart, as working for the Lord, not for men." So, how do you see your daily life? Is it a series of mundane tasks or a meaningful calling? Do you strive to please people, or is your ultimate aim to honor God? By keeping our eyes on Him, we can rise above the temptation to seek approval from others and instead reflect His goodness and grace in all areas of life. Live with excellence, knowing that your efforts, done for God's glory, have eternal value. Today, let's live with purpose, working wholeheartedly for the Lord.

**Journal:** Are you more focused on pleasing people or honoring God? Reflect on how Colossians 3:23 challenges you to see your daily life as a meaningful calling rather than a routine.

**One-sentence prayer:** Heavenly Father, I'm living for You today.

***Further hope and encouragement: Colossians 3***

## DAY 8

# Translation

*Therefore, my dear friends, as you have always obeyed—not only in
my presence, but how much more in my absence—continue to
work out your salvation with fear and trembling, for it is God
who works in you to will and to act according to his good purpose.*
*Philippians 2:12-13*

There are many translations of the New Testament—in fact, there are over one hundred English translations. That's a lot of translations! Harry Ironside (Ironside, as cited in various sources) once shared that the best translation of the New Testament was the way his mom lived her life. Wow. Let's pause right there for a moment. As a longtime preacher of the Word of God, Ironside pointed to his mother as someone who truly followed Jesus and lived out the Word of God. What an incredible legacy to leave for the people in your life: living out the Word of God.

The way we live speaks volumes about what we truly believe. We've discussed it before, but we are called to be doers of the Word. We can have all the Biblical knowledge in the world, but if it's not reflected in the way we live, what use is it? Do we point people closer to Jesus, or do we pull them away by the way we live—our words, reactions, decisions, and responses? What we say or don't say is important, but even more crucial is the way we live—because that is the translation of the Bible that others see. Do we have Scripture memorized in our minds, but it doesn't make its way to our hearts and out through our hands, feet, and mouth? It's not about knowing the Bible; it's about living it. Like Ironside's mother, what an awesome legacy it would be if you, _____, were the best translation of the Bible anyone ever "read." Imagine the impact we could have if our lives reflected God's love and truth every day, showing the world who Jesus is through our actions.

**Journal:** How can you be a living translation of God's Word to the people around you? Reflect on how your actions, words, and character reflect the teachings of Scripture in your daily life.

**One-sentence prayer:** Heavenly Father, help me to live out Your Word in such a way that others see You through me.

**Further hope and encouragement: Philippians 2:12-18**

# DAY 9
# Quiet the Noise

*Let the morning bring me word of your unfailing love, for I have put my trust in you. Show me the way I should go, for to you I entrust my life.*
*Psalm 143:8*

How do you start your day? Do you wake up and immediately check your inbox as you're lying in bed? Is the first thing you do in the morning scroll through social media? Do you turn on the television or read the news? Do you see text messages on your screen and feel the need to respond right away? If you're anything like me, you're faced daily with the feeling of waking up and seeing what's waiting for you. The moment I touch my phone—even if it's just to turn off the alarm—I feel the pull of distraction. The noise of the day rushes in the instant I see a message, an email, or anything from the outside world.

Psalm 143:8 reminds us of a better way to begin. The psalmist prays, "Let the morning bring me word of your unfailing love, for I have put my trust in you. Show me the way I should go, for to you I entrust my life." Before the noise, the to-dos, and the pressures of the day take hold, the psalmist shows us how to quiet our hearts and seek God's guidance. Mornings are a fresh opportunity to entrust your life, your plans, and your worries to the One who holds the day. Start with Him. Let His unfailing love anchor your heart, and let His direction shape your path. There's going to be plenty of noise today—why not start by listening to the voice that matters most? Spending time with Jesus to start each day will quiet the noise headed your way.

**Journal:** How do you start your day, and how might that affect your ability to live with clarity and peace? Reflect on your current morning routine and how distractions might hinder your focus. What can you do to prioritize quiet time with God so you can begin each day grounded and ready to live with purpose?

**One-sentence prayer:** Heavenly Father, quiet the noise today.

*Further hope and encouragement: Psalm 143*

## DAY 10
# Lift Your Eyes

*I lift my eyes to the hills—where does my help come from?*
*My help comes from the Lord, the Maker of Heaven and Earth.*
*Psalm 121:1*

We live in a world and society where we're looking down more and more every day. Have you ever heard of nomophobia? It's a psychological condition where people fear being without a mobile phone. We've developed the habit of looking down at the device in our hands. I'm guilty. I often allow my phone to steal my gaze. Before I know it, every spare second I have is filled with my eyes looking down, habitually opening and closing apps for no reason at all. When I pull up to a red light, my eyes look down at my phone. When I'm standing in a line, here comes my phone. When I get to work and walk from my car to the building, where do I look? My phone.

All these tiny habits of looking down steal my gaze from looking up. They rob me of the opportunity to fix my mind on things above (Colossians 3:2) and instead draw me toward earthly distractions. Psalm 121:1 reminds us, "I lift my eyes to the hills—where does my help come from? My help comes from the Lord, the Maker of heaven and earth." Notice the verse doesn't say "look down." It says, "I lift my eyes." And who does the psalmist lift their eyes to? "The Lord, the Maker of heaven and earth." Identify the moments when you're in the habit of looking down at your phone, and turn them into moments of looking up. Let those brief pauses in your day be opportunities to connect with God instead of distractions. In a world looking down, lift your eyes today.

**Journal:** Take a moment to reflect on your daily habits. How often do you find yourself looking down—whether at your phone or other distractions? How can you intentionally lift your eyes to God in these moments? Write about times today when you can shift your focus from the earthly to the eternal and trust that your help comes from the Lord.

**One-sentence prayer:** Heavenly Father, I lift my eyes to You today.

**Further hope and encouragement: Psalm 121**

# DAY 11
# Ambassadors

*We are therefore Christ's ambassadors, as though*
*God were making his appeal through us.*
*2 Corinthians 5:20*

Leaving my house as a teenager, my dad would often say, "Remember who you are and who you represent." And you know how things work—before long, we start to sound like our parents. I now find myself saying the same thing to my kids as they leave the house or I drop them off somewhere. My dad's words were a reminder to be an ambassador for Jesus. The role of an ambassador is to represent something greater than oneself. Unfortunately, instead of adopting an ambassador mentality in our daily lives, we often take an ownership approach, living for ourselves. We can too easily drift toward pursuing our needs, our wants, our desires—chasing after our own agendas and forgetting that our lives belong to Christ.

Paul reminds us in 2 Corinthians 5:20 that "we are therefore Christ's ambassadors." This truth should transform how we approach each day—every thought, every interaction, every conversation, every decision, and every action. Our calling as followers of Jesus is to reflect His character in both our words and our actions. Everything we do—how we respond, how we serve, how we love—is significant because we represent Jesus. We must surrender the idea that our lives are about us and instead embrace the mission of living as Christ's ambassadors—all the time, everywhere, no matter where we are or what we do. Remember, Jesus didn't come to do His own will, but the will of the One who sent Him. So today, take a moment to pause and reflect: remember who you are and Who you represent.

**Journal:** How can you better reflect the character of Jesus in your daily life? Identify one specific situation or relationship where you can intentionally act as His ambassador this week.

**One-sentence prayer:** Heavenly Father, it's You that I'm representing today.

*Further hope and encouragement: 2 Corinthians 5*

# DAY 12
# Close the Gap

*Do not merely listen to the word, and so deceive yourselves.*
*Do what it says.*
*James 1:22*

We often hear about the importance of closing the "say-do" gap in life and leadership—the disconnect between what someone says they'll do and what actually happens. It's that subtle but powerful space between words and actions. I remember a former superintendent who once wrote me a letter of recommendation. He prided himself on closing the say-do gap. "If I say I'm going to do something, I'm going to do it," he often said. True to his word, when I gave him a date by which I needed the letter, he asked for the deadline and promised to have it done. As the day approached, I considered sending a reminder—but sure enough, right on time, the letter arrived in my inbox with a simple note: "If I say I'm going to do it, I'm going to do it."

That moment stuck with me. It was a small gesture, but it revealed a bigger truth: integrity shows up in the little things, and our actions should consistently reflect our words. James 1:22 calls us to close another important gap—the "hear-do" gap: Do not merely listen to the word, and so deceive yourselves. Do what it says. It's not enough to just listen to God's Word or know what it says. We're called to live it out. To forgive when it's hard. To show compassion when we feel empty. To pursue peace when conflict would be easier. To love the unlovable. The Bible isn't just something to *read*—it's something to *do*. All of us face moments when living out our faith feels inconvenient, challenging, or even risky. But that's when it matters most. So today, let's commit not just to being hearers of the Word—but doers. Let's close the gap.

**Journal:** What specific step can you take this week to align your actions with what God's Word is calling you to do? Is there an area where your hearing and doing need to reconnect?

**One-sentence prayer:** Heavenly Father, help me not only to hear Your Word but to live it out each day in both my words and actions.

***Further hope and encouragement: James 1***

# DAY 13
# As For Me and My House

*But as for me and my household, we will serve the Lord.*
*Joshua 24:15*

I can still hear my wife, Carly's, words: "Zac, do you want our family to fall apart? Because that's exactly what's happening. We're falling apart. The kids need you, I need you. Are things ever going to change? I'm tired of this." To make matters worse, this wasn't the first time I had heard similar words from her. I was headed for disaster and didn't even realize it. I was destroying my home, my marriage, and my relationship with the kids one day at a time. I was exhausted, missing dinner at home, getting caught up on work during the weekends, laptop always out.

I'm sick and tired of watching people pour everything they have into their careers, hobbies, or responsibilities while missing the mark at home. I'm tired of seeing families struggle because priorities are out of order. And of course, I'm speaking to myself here as well. If we're thriving in our work, social circles, or personal pursuits but neglecting the people who need us most, then we're missing the point. One of my favorite quotes is from Mother Teresa (n.d): "If you want to change the world, go home and love your family." That doesn't mean we stop striving for excellence in what we do, but when the day is over, we must go home and be fully present with the ones God has entrusted to us. What we need are more people committed to making their homes a place that honors God. We can't serve Him in our families if we're not truly present in them. Dear friend, you are replaceable at work, in your community, and even in your social circles—but not at home. Go home, serve the Lord, and love your family well, for that is where your greatest impact begins.

**Journal:** Think about your current rhythm between work, responsibilities, and home life. Are there any areas where you might be neglecting your family in pursuit of other things? How can you make more time to serve and love your family well?

**One-sentence prayer:** Heavenly Father, as for me and my house, we will serve You.

***Further hope and encouragement: Joshua 24, Psalm 128***

## DAY 14
# Toward the Goal

*I press on toward the goal to win the prize for which*
*God has called me heavenward in Christ Jesus.*
*Philippians 3:14*

I live in Lancaster County, Pennsylvania, where there is a large Amish population—and with the Amish come Amish buggies on the roads. Fun fact: between October and December, it's Amish wedding season, and on Tuesdays and Thursdays, buggies are everywhere. These buggies are typically pulled by horses, and if you look closely, you'll notice that the horses wear blinders on the sides of their eyes. Blinders limit a horse's peripheral vision and help it focus on its task—getting the buggy safely from one place to another. By restricting its view, the blinders reduce distractions and prevent the horse from getting spooked. When buggies are pulled by two horses, the blinders also help the horses avoid being distracted by one another. Interestingly, racehorses wear blinders, too (often called "blinkers"). In that setting, blinders improve performance by helping the horse concentrate solely on the track ahead, rather than the noise or motion of competitors.

In Philippians 3:14, Paul writes, "I press on toward the goal to win the prize for which God has called me heavenward in Christ Jesus." As followers of Jesus, we know our purpose is to glorify God and enjoy Him forever. Yet too often, we allow distractions to pull our focus away. The world offers many temptations—praise from others, social media validation, comparison, approval, success. Even the good gifts God gives us can become distractions if we elevate them above His calling on our lives. Here's the thing: Just like a horse needs blinders to stay on course, we too must keep our eyes fixed on what matters most. Let's press on toward the goal, keeping our gaze on the prize God has set before us, refusing to be sidetracked by the noise and distractions that surround us.

**Journal:** When have distractions pulled you away from what matters most? What "blinders" can help you stay focused on your purpose?

**One-sentence prayer:** Heavenly Father, help keep my eyes focused on You and the calling You've placed on my life.

***Further hope and encouragement: Philippians 3***

## DAY 15
# Wake Up Earlier

*Very early in the morning while it was still dark, Jesus got up, left the house and went off to a solitary place where he prayed.*
*Mark 1:35*

A word we often use in conversation is "busy." How are things going? "Oh, it's a busy season right now." How was your week? "It was a busy one." What's the week ahead looking like? "Busy." Everyone is busy, busy, busy. I was sitting in a Sunday School class on spiritual disciplines when the topic of time—or the lack thereof—came up. An older man in the class shared something profound that I'll always carry with me. He said, "As I've journeyed through life and various seasons, as I took on more responsibilities and time seemed to disappear, I woke up earlier." He went on to explain that no matter what stage of life he was in, he woke up earlier and earlier to spend time with his Heavenly Father.

Maybe you're struggling to find the time to meet with God, thinking, "I just don't have the time!" Let me be straightforward today—make the time. Wake up earlier. I often share this, but as the attention on Jesus grew and crowds followed Him—wanting to be healed by Him, listen to His teaching, or simply be in His presence—Jesus never said, "I'm too busy to spend time with my Father." Instead, He made it a priority to spend the first part of His day with His Father. As Mark 1:35 reminds us: "Very early in the morning, while it was still dark, Jesus got up, left the house and went off to a solitary place, where He prayed." I'm sure your life is "busy," but we should never be too busy for our Heavenly Father. Are you struggling to find time to be alone with God? Make the time by waking up very early in the morning, while it's still dark. Your Father is waiting for you.

**Journal:** What steps can you take to carve out intentional time with God, even during a busy season of life? How might waking up earlier change your day?

**One-sentence prayer:** Heavenly Father, help me to seek You first, even when life feels busy.

**Further hope and encouragement: Luke 5**

# DAY 16
# Seven Minutes

*Now when Daniel learned that the decree had been published,*
*he went home to his upstairs room where the windows opened*
*toward Jerusalem. Three times a day he got down on his knees and*
*prayed, giving thanks to his God, just as he had done before.*
*Daniel 6:10*

My pastor shared a story about one of his seminary professors. The professor challenged the class to start with just seven minutes a day. Seven minutes for what, you may ask? Start with seven minutes for Bible reading and prayer. The professor encouraged the class to read the Bible for four minutes and spend three minutes in prayer. Some in the class were already well past seven minutes, others were sporadic—they read their Bible and prayed some days, but not others. And some struggled with where to start. Sounds a lot like exercise, doesn't it? God's Word is a lamp unto our feet and a light unto our path (Psalm 119:105). We are called to meditate on His Word day and night (Psalm 1:2) and pray without ceasing (1 Thessalonians 5:17).

Here's the thing: It's the "little" things, done consistently, that lead to results. When I talk about results in today's devotion, I'm referring to heart transformation. Reflect honestly: How are your Bible reading and prayer habits? Maybe you're going well past seven minutes. Maybe you're struggling to get started because you think you need to start with a large chunk of time. Instead of spending any quiet time with God, you end up spending none. Here's my challenge to you: Start with seven minutes a day. I'll tweak the formula a little bit. I recommend doing this in the morning, but find what works best for you. Will you start your day with these seven minutes? Set an alarm for the middle of your day? Or end your day with seven minutes? You could even look to Daniel's example of praying three times a day (Daniel 6:10) and incorporate these seven minutes at different points in your day. Start with Bible reading for three minutes, hearing what God has to say through His Word. Then, spend one minute in silent meditation or journaling whatever thoughts come to mind. Lastly, spend three minutes turning what you read and meditated on into prayer. Seven minutes. Start there, and watch what happens.

**Journal:** Take a moment to reflect on your current Bible reading and prayer habits. What might it look like to start with just seven minutes a day?

How could this small commitment lead to greater transformation in your relationship with God?

**One-sentence prayer:** Heavenly Father, help me to carve out time each day to connect with You through Your Word and prayer, trusting that even the smallest moments spent with You will transform my heart.

*Further hope and encouragement: Daniel 6*

# DAY 17
# Meditate

*But his delight is on the law of the Lord and*
*on his law he mediates day and night.*
*Psalm 1:2*

What do you think about all day? What fills your mind and heart, and ultimately comes out through your words and actions? Often, we move so quickly from one task to another—physically and mentally—that we don't take the time to pause and reflect. Let's define meditation: The world often encourages emptying our minds, but Christian meditation is the intentional filling of our minds with God and His truths found in Scripture. Thomas Manton (2000) said, "The Word feeds meditation, and meditation feeds prayer...meditation must follow hearing and precede prayer... What we take in by the Word we digest by meditation and let out by prayer."

As the Psalmist says in Psalm 1:2, "But his delight is in the law of the Lord, and on His law he meditates day and night." Our hearts and minds need to be filled with the Word of God so that day and night, Scripture fills our thoughts. We need to absorb the Scriptures—not just read them quickly in the morning and forget them by midday. What overflows from us will be revealed in the way we live, the way we speak, and how we interact and treat others. Whether we're in the car, at work, or walking through our day, let's make it a point to recite Scripture throughout the day. Let God's Word guide us and shape our lives as we meditate on it today.

**Journal:** Take a moment to reflect on the last few days. What thoughts have dominated your mind, and how have they influenced your actions? What Scripture could you meditate on to shift your focus back to God's truth? Write about how you can intentionally incorporate time for reflection and meditation on God's Word into your daily routine.

**One-sentence prayer:** Heavenly Father, help me fix my thoughts on You.

*Further hope and encouragement: Psalm 1*

# DAY 18
# Grace Wins Every Time

*When you were dead in your sins and in the uncircumcision of
your sinful nature, God made you alive with Christ. He forgave all
our sins, having canceled the written code, with its regulations, that was
against us and stood opposed to us; he took it away, nailing it to a cross.*
*Colossians 2:13-14*

I had the opportunity to travel to San Quentin Rehabilitation Center in California with Bob Goff and Jody Luke as part of the *Love Does* San Quentin Prison Program. While leading a small group in the chapel, one inmate said something I'll never forget. This man had been in prison for nearly fifteen years and likely wasn't getting out. He found Jesus in his jail cell and shared the following: "The moment I said sorry to God and asked for forgiveness, He forgave me. But for years, I struggled to forgive myself. I've learned that when I don't forgive myself, I'm making myself bigger than God." He went on to say that while the world may see a debt against him, because of Jesus, that debt has already been paid.

Here's the thing: when we confess our sins and wrongdoings to God, He forgives us—right then and there. We are forgiven because of Jesus' death on the cross and His resurrection. I don't know what pain or regrets you're holding onto today, but let them go to Jesus. Paul Tripp (2014) puts it beautifully: "Grace forces you to feel the pain of your regrets, but never asks you to pay for them, because the price has already been paid by Jesus." Rest in the truth from Colossians: we were dead in our sins, but God made us alive with Christ. He forgave all our sins, canceled our record of wrongs, and nailed it to the cross (v.13-14). That doesn't mean our sins and mistakes don't have earthly consequences—they do. But always remember this: Jesus already paid the price on the cross, and grace wins every time.

**Journal:** What is one area of your life where you struggle to accept God's forgiveness? Write a prayer asking God to help you fully receive His grace and let go of shame or guilt.

**One-sentence prayer:** Heavenly Father, thank You for sending your Son, Jesus, to pay the price I could never pay—help me live each day in the freedom of Your grace.

*Further hope and encouragement: Matthew 27:32-56, Colossians 2*

## DAY 19

# Throw the "Cupcakes" Out

*Why spend money on what is not bread, and your labor on*
*what does not satisfy? Listen, listen to me, and eat what is good,*
*and your soul will delight in the richest of fare.*
Isaiah 55:2

Carly, Olivia, and I traveled to Florida one April to visit my grandparents, Me-Me and Pap-Pap, in St. Petersburg. They lived in Pennsylvania but spent their winters in Florida. Let me tell you something—Me-Me can cook! Some of my favorite memories are sitting around the table with family, enjoying her wonderful meals. One day during our trip, we spent time at St. Pete Beach before heading back to their house shortly before dinner. I was pumped for the meal Me-Me was making: roast beef, mashed potatoes, and corn—one of her signature dishes. About forty-five minutes before dinner, a box of beautiful store-bought cupcakes caught my eye. Like a five-year-old, I stared at them for a while, thinking, "I shouldn't...it's almost dinner time." Then, I rationalized, "OK, just one." Minutes later, all twelve cupcakes were gone. (Hey, they were mini.) The next thing I heard was Me-Me's voice: "Dinner's ready!" It was time for the meal I had been looking forward to all day, but guess what? My stomach hurt a little. I wasn't hungry. I had lost my appetite.

Here's the question I want to ask you: What's impacting your appetite for the Lord? Like my mini cupcakes in Florida, what's causing you to lose your hunger for Jesus? There was a feast prepared for me, but I chose the temporary—the quick fix—and it ruined my ability to enjoy the goodness of the roast beef, mashed potatoes, and corn. So, what is it for you? Is it the approval of others? The desire to be accepted? A relationship? Social media? Technology? Maybe it's something else. Whatever it is, name it today. Maybe it's a whole lot of things, but start with one. The truth is, we often settle for things that don't truly satisfy when God has something so much better for us. Isaiah 55:2 says, "Why spend money on what is not bread, and your labor on what does not satisfy? Listen, listen to me, and eat what is good, and your soul will delight in the richest of fare." We serve a wonderful, merciful, compassionate Father who knows what's best for our lives. Throw the "cupcakes" out today and taste what God has for you.

**Journal:** What are the "cupcakes" in your life—things that seem appealing in the moment but leave you feeling empty? How can you refocus your appetite on the things of God?

**One-sentence prayer:** Heavenly Father, help me recognize the things that are distracting me from You, and give me the strength to choose what truly satisfies

*Further hope and encouragement: Isaiah 55, Matthew 4:1-11*

## DAY 20
# Comforting Others

*Praise be to the God and Father of our Lord Jesus Christ, the
Father of compassion and the God of all comfort, who comforts
us in all our troubles, so that we can comfort those in any
trouble with the comfort we ourselves receive from God.*
*2 Corinthians 1:3-4*

Human beings are wired to connect. Have you ever waved or given a slight head nod to someone driving the same car as yours? I don't know why, but there's something about that shared connection. One day, I was talking to someone and we realized we had the same dentist, which led to a laugh and a fist bump. A friend of mine once shared how he feels a special connection to anyone who eats plain cheeseburgers, just like him. These are silly examples, but they show how much we're built for connection, even in small ways.

I vividly remember my season of anxiety and depression. At church, I heard a man share about his own battle, and his words mirrored exactly what I was feeling. That connection gave me the courage to reach out and talk to him. He encouraged me to open up about my struggles, which I had kept hidden because I thought I was alone. God used that difficult season not only to draw me closer to Him but also to show me the power of connection in helping others. Our struggles and experiences can be bridges to others. When we open up and share, we reflect God's comfort and grace, drawing people closer to Him. Who can you reach out to this week and remind them that they're not alone? Let's comfort others because of the comfort we've been given.

**Journal:** Who can you connect with this week by sharing part of your story, and how might it strengthen your relationships?

**One-sentence prayer:** Heavenly Father, help me to lead with vulnerability, sharing Your love and compassion with those I encounter.

***Further hope and encouragement: 2 Corinthians 1***

# DAY 21
# Leading as Sheep

*I am sending you out like sheep among wolves.*
*Therefore, be as shrewd as snakes and as innocent as doves.*
*Matthew 10:16*

We've all heard it said: "Be a leader, not a follower." It's a phrase meant to inspire confidence and independence. But what if the key to living well wasn't about leading first, but following? There's much written about shepherds, but leadership begins with recognizing our identity as sheep. David, one of the most well-known shepherds in Scripture, first acknowledged his own vulnerability and need. When he declared, "The Lord is my Shepherd," he recognized that, like a sheep, he was dependent, prone to wander, and in constant need of guidance. This humble acknowledgment became the foundation of his strength and trust in God.

As sheep, we're reminded of our need to rely on our Shepherd for direction, protection, and provision. Jesus Himself sends us out as "sheep among wolves," calling us to face life's challenges with a balance of wisdom and purity. Recognizing this identity helps us live with humility, understanding that we can't navigate life's uncertainties on our own. By embracing our role as sheep, we find freedom. Instead of trying to control every outcome or shoulder every burden, we can rest in the care of the Good Shepherd. He sees the dangers we cannot, provides the strength we lack, and offers peace when life feels overwhelming. Today, lean into your dependence on Him—because true strength is found in knowing Who we follow.

**Journal:** Reflect on how your dependence on God impacts the way you approach life. What areas are you trying to control on your own? How can you embrace the freedom of trusting Him more fully today?

**One-sentence prayer:** Heavenly Father, help me embrace my identity as Your sheep, trusting in Your guidance and care as I navigate life.

***Further hope and encouragement: Matthew 10***

# DAY 22
# Quick to Listen

*My dear brothers, take note of this: Everyone should be*
*quick to listen, slow to speak, and slow to become angry.*
*James 1:19*

I was in a meeting that included a child's parent and four members of the school team. The parent's frustration grew throughout the meeting until she eventually lashed out, raising her voice and swearing at the team multiple times. In her frustration, she said, "I feel like no one is listening to me." At that moment, a team member stopped her and began answering her questions. She stood up, shared a couple more expletives, and stormed out of the room. A few hours later, that same team member came to me and said, "That was my fault. At that moment this morning she didn't need an answer, she just wanted to be heard." He went on to reflect that the timing of his response was poor.

We often have the tendency to try and "fix" things, but as this individual learned from the meeting, sometimes people don't need an answer—they just want to be heard. James reminds us that we should be quick to listen and slow to speak (James 1:19). I'm not pointing the finger at the person in the story above—I've been there many times. Often, I'll cut Carly off before she's done talking, and she'll say, "I'm not done, I just need you to listen." It's easy to feel the need to provide quick solutions, but sometimes the most important thing we can offer is our full attention. Being slow to speak and quick to listen allows us to truly understand the heart of the matter and shows that we value the person in front of us. May we live with ears that are open and words that are few. Be quick to listen and slow to speak today.

**Journal:** Think about a recent conversation where you may have been quick to respond rather than truly listening. How did that impact the outcome? Reflect on a situation today where you can be "quick to listen and slow to speak." How might this approach help you understand others better and live with greater empathy?

**One-sentence prayer:** Heavenly Father, help me be quick to listen and slow to speak today.

***Further hope and encouragement: James 1***

# DAY 23
# Exactly Who I Am

*The good man brings good things out of the good stored up in his heart,*
*and the evil man brings evil things out of the evil stored up in his heart.*
*For out of the overflow of his heart his mouth speaks.*
*Luke 6:45*

I've had many conversations with kids who've gotten themselves into trouble. Here are two things I've learned. First, when confronted about what they did, their initial response is to point to someone else and explain why that person caused them to act as they did. "I hit him because he…" or "I said that because she…" Second, I've learned that I am more like those kids pointing fingers than I'd like to imagine. When something happens in my life, I am quick to point externally to why it occurred instead of looking internally at why I responded the way I did.

Have you ever reacted harshly and done something you regret, then followed it up with, "I'm sorry about _____. I don't know why I did that; that's not who I am"? Here's the thing (and I'm talking to myself, too): that's exactly who you are, and that's exactly who I am. As Luke 6:45 states, we bring outside of us what is stored inside of us. The way we respond—our words and our actions—are an overflow of our hearts. The way we live externally reflects the condition of our hearts internally. It's not the people or situations that cause us to respond poorly; rather, those moments reveal what's already inside us. The next time you're ready to say, "That's not who I am," replace it with, "That's exactly who I am," and run to the never-ending grace and mercy of the Heavenly Father.

**Journal:** How do you typically respond when things don't go as planned or when you feel challenged? Reflect on today's verse, Luke 6:45. What do your reactions reveal about what's stored in your heart? How can you align your heart with the values and principles you want to reflect in your life?

**One-sentence prayer:** Heavenly Father, You know exactly who I am.

***Further hope and encouragement: Luke 6:43-45***

# DAY 24

# Live with Contentment

*But godliness with contentment is great gain.*
*1 Timothy 6:6*

Many of us live with "an itch for more." The drive for accomplishment can push us to seek promotions, recognition, praise, acceptance, or influence. I've struggled with contentment myself—feeling that no matter what I do, it's never enough. The truth is, when we pursue success and accolades on our own terms, we often find that achieving more doesn't fulfill our deepest needs. Paul reminds us in 1 Timothy, "But godliness with contentment is great gain. For we brought nothing into this world, and we can take nothing out of it" (1 Timothy 6:6-7). As is often quoted, "I have never seen a U-Haul behind a hearse."

Let's shift our perspective. We must not put our hope in the fleeting things of this world. Instead, as Paul advises, let's put our hope in God, "who richly provides everything for our enjoyment" (1 Timothy 6:17). Only in doing so can we "take hold of the life that is truly life" (1 Timothy 6:19). So today, instead of striving for more titles, influence, or wealth, let's fill in the blank: "But you, _____, flee from all of this and pursue righteousness, godliness, faith, love, endurance, and gentleness. Fight the good fight of faith" (1 Timothy 6:11-12). Our true legacy is found not in what we accumulate, but in how we live with integrity, faith, and godliness. Let's pursue the things that have eternal value and live with contentment.

**Journal:** What are you chasing in life that might be distracting you from living with contentment in God? How can you shift your focus today to pursue righteousness, godliness, and faith over worldly achievements?

**One-sentence prayer:** Heavenly Father, help me to live with contentment and focus on what truly matters: You.

*Further hope and encouragement: Ecclesiastes 1, 1 Timothy 6*

## DAY 25
# Not My Will, But Yours Be Done

*For I have come down from heaven not to do my*
*will but to do the will of him who sent me.*
*John 6:38*

We often seek advice on how to improve—whether it's through self-help books, podcasts, or online tips offering strategies to live better, grow stronger, look for quick fixes, or navigate life's challenges. But living well isn't about mastering the latest techniques. It's about following our Heavenly Father through Jesus Christ and aligning our lives with His purpose. The question we should be asking isn't, "What's the best strategy?" but rather, "What is God's view of what He's called me to do?" Too often, we approach life as if we're in control—"my plans, my family, my goals." But the truth is, it's all God's. Recognizing this can stop us in our tracks. True fulfillment begins when we humbly acknowledge that our lives, our families, our time, and everything we do belong to Him. God has entrusted us with these blessings, not for our purposes, but for His kingdom. When we see life in this light, we live with humility, knowing it's all for God's glory, not our own.

Jesus, the ultimate example, came from heaven to earth to show us the way, and His mission culminated in His sacrifice on the cross. In John 6:38, Jesus said, "For I have come down from heaven not to do my will but to do the will of him who sent me." This statement reflects the heart of a life well-lived—seeking God's will above our own. Our journey begins by knowing who we are in Christ. When we align our identity with Him, it transforms how we live and impacts those around us. So today, like Jesus, let's say, Not my will, but Yours be done.

**Journal:** How can you align your actions with God's will rather than your own? Reflect on the blessings and responsibilities God has entrusted to you—how does seeing them as His change your perspective? What steps can you take this week to live with humility and purpose, seeking God's glory above all?

**One-sentence prayer:** Heavenly Father, not my will, but Yours be done today.

*Further hope and encouragement: Psalm 40*

## DAY 26

# Weak and Vulnerable

*The second angel said to him: "Run, tell that young man,*
*'Jerusalem will be a city without walls because of the great number*
*of people and animals in it. And I myself will be a wall of fire*
*around it,' declares the Lord, 'and I will be its glory within.'"*
*Zechariah 2:4-5*

As human beings, we don't wake up feeling the same every day. Some days we feel strong and confident; other days, we wake up feeling vulnerable and fragile. If we're honest, vulnerability creeps in more often than we'd like to admit. There are times when we feel like there's no way we can make it through the day. It's a feeling of doubt and worry—whether from past struggles, stress, looming responsibilities, or uncertainty about what's ahead. Sometimes, we can't even pinpoint the cause; we're just worn down. It's as if, at any moment, we could be paralyzed by fear, stuck in bed or at our devotionals, unable to move forward.

But here's the truth—God provides the strength we need for each day. There are times when we feel like running away from it all, wishing for simpler, quieter moments. Yet, in those moments of weakness, God is there, lifting us up and carrying us through. Just like He promised to protect Jerusalem with His mighty presence, He is our wall of fire, protecting and surrounding us with His strength. As John Piper (2020) says, "If you wake up feeling fragile, remember that God is not, and then trust Him to be everything you need today."

**Journal:** Think about a time when you collectively or personally felt completely overwhelmed by life's demands. How did God provide strength for you in that moment? Write down ways you can rely on Him more fully the next time you feel weak or vulnerable.

**One-sentence prayer:** Heavenly Father, help me today, You are the wall of fire around me.

*Further hope and encouragement: Zechariah 2*

# DAY 27
# Giving Our Best

*Whatever your hand finds to do, do it with all your might.*
*Ecclesiastes 9:10*

One evening after school, I sat in my office finishing up emails before heading home. Richard, the evening custodian, came in to empty the trash. I always enjoy these end-of-day conversations with custodians—you never know what life stories or wisdom they'll share. That day, I complimented Richard on his hard work and mentioned some positive feedback I'd received from staff. Richard smiled and said something I'll never forget: "My motto is, whatever work I'm asked to do, I'm going to give it my best." Richard's role is one that often went unnoticed: emptying trash, sweeping floors, and vacuuming carpets after everyone else had left. But his attitude inspired me deeply: no matter the task, he chose to give his best.

Ecclesiastes 9:10 reminds us, "Whatever your hand finds to do, do it with all your might." This verse teaches us that all work—no matter how mundane or unseen—has value for God's glory. Every task we've been called to do is an opportunity to serve Him and reflect His goodness in our lives. Mundane tasks—folding laundry, washing dishes, leading meetings, or responding to emails, difficult parenting days — can feel repetitive and insignificant. God sees our faithfulness in the everyday, even when no one else does. Richard's motto challenges us to embrace every task with diligence and urgency, giving our best in all we're called to do. Whether preparing dinner, showing kindness to a coworker, or tackling a to-do list, we're called to work with excellence—not for praise, but as an offering to God. Next time a task feels insignificant, remember Richard's example and Ecclesiastes 9:10. Whatever God places before you today, give it your best.

**Journal:** What tasks in your daily life, whether at home or work, feel small or mundane? How can you shift your mindset to view them as acts of worship and opportunities to glorify God?

**One-sentence prayer:** Heavenly Father, help me give my best in all that I do, even in the small and unseen tasks, for Your glory.

***Further hope and encouragement: Ecclesiastes 9***

# DAY 28
# Identity Crisis

*For in Him we live and move and have our being.*
*Acts 17:28*

Another school year had come to an end, and it was the first day of summer break. As I sat in the office, I remember feeling empty. The school year had been challenging, yet fulfilling—each day filled with purpose, energy, and momentum. But now, with the halls quiet and people gone, I felt a strange void. Olympic athletes experience a similar struggle. After years of preparation, discipline, and sacrifice, they step onto the world's biggest stage. Yet, when the games end, many are left wondering, *Who am I now?* With their identity tied to their achievements, the loss of purpose post-competition often leads to feelings of emptiness. Without the familiar rhythm of training and competing, athletes can struggle to find a sense of direction as they return home. We may not all be Olympians, but we've likely felt this tension too—after the completion of a big project, the end of a season, or a significant life change. It's the "letdown effect"—when our bodies, minds, and emotions crash, leaving us vulnerable to illness, anxiety, and sadness. These moments expose the truth: if our identity is wrapped up in what we do, then who are we when the doing stops?

The good news is that our identity isn't found in temporary achievements or roles here on earth. Acts 17:28 reminds us, "For in Him we live and move and have our being." Our true identity is not in what we accomplish but in who we belong to—Christ. When we place our worth in Him, we are freed from the exhausting cycle of proving ourselves. Our identity is rooted in His unchanging love, not in how well we perform or what goals we meet. Even when seasons shift and our roles change, we remain children of God, secure in His grace. If you're feeling lost after a transition or battling a sense of purposelessness, lean into Jesus. You are not defined by what you do—you're defined by Who you belong to. In Christ, you have value and purpose, no matter what stage or season of life you are in.

**Journal:** Where are you finding your identity right now—in your roles, achievements, or in Christ? Reflect on how you can place your sense of worth on being a child of God, regardless of your circumstances.

**One-sentence prayer:** Heavenly Father, help me rest in the truth that my identity is found in You, not in what I do.

*Further hope and encouragement: Acts 17:24-28, Psalm 139:13-14*

# DAY 29
# Never Alone

*The Lord himself goes before you and will be with you; he will never leave you nor forsake you. Do not be afraid; do not be discouraged.*
*Deuteronomy 31:8*

I remember talking to a friend starting a new job after twelve years in a different place. On the first day, sitting in their new office, they were overwhelmed by doubt and uncertainty. They described those moments as some of the loneliest they had ever felt. The relationships they had built over the years seemed so distant, and the thought of starting over felt daunting. They questioned why they had left the familiar for the unknown. But in the stillness, they whispered aloud, "God is with me," and suddenly felt a wave of peace and confidence. In that moment, they remembered the powerful truth: no matter where we go, God is always with us.

When Moses prepared Joshua to succeed him as leader of the Israelites, he offered these comforting words: "The Lord himself goes before you and will be with you; he will never leave you nor forsake you. Do not be afraid; do not be discouraged" (Deuteronomy 31:8). These words weren't just for Joshua—they are for all of us. Are you stepping into the unknown? Feeling overwhelmed by a tough decision or a change in your life? Maybe you feel isolated in your daily tasks or unsure of what lies ahead. Whatever you're facing, take heart in this truth: God goes with you, and He goes before you. Not only does God promise His presence, but He equips you for the journey. Trust that He is already preparing the way, providing what you need for each step. As Moses told Joshua, you are never alone. In every moment—whether exciting or challenging—God walks beside you, leading and strengthening you for the road ahead.

**Journal:** Think about a time when you felt unsure or alone. How did God remind you of His presence? What step can you take today to trust Him more in your journey?

**One-sentence prayer:** Heavenly Father, You are with me, I am never alone.

*Further hope and encouragement: Deuteronomy 31*

# DAY 30
# Pure Joy

*Consider it pure joy, my brothers, when you face trials of many kinds.*
*James 1:2*

What comes to mind when you hear the words "pure joy?" When I think of pure joy, I think of pizza and ice cream. I think of cheeseburgers and French fries. I think of winning, success, celebrations, and everything going as planned. I picture a baseball player rounding third base after hitting a walk-off home run in the last inning, with his team waiting to celebrate at home plate. I think of March Madness. When I think of pure joy, I envision a day when everything is going right—my family is happy, the kids are listening, teachers and students are positive, and everyone is walking around with that Friday feeling, fist-bumping one another as we head into the weekend.

Not so fast. James tells us to consider it pure joy when we "face trials of many kinds" (James 1:2). And let's be honest—life is filled with trials. So how do we respond? With grumbling and complaining, or do we consider them pure joy? Here's the thing about challenges—they shape us. The difficulties we face are all part of God's plan. Not only do we battle our own struggles and challenges, but we also walk alongside others in their struggles and challenges. God uses the trials in our lives to help us surrender to Him, realizing we can't do it on our own. These hardships were ordained by God to soften and shape our hearts, smoothing out the rough edges like sandpaper. Maybe the trials you're facing have you ready to give up or look for an easier path. Don't give up. Do not be discouraged. See God's grace through your trials and trust that He is using them to produce character that wouldn't grow in a life of ease. Consider your trials pure joy today.

**Journal:** Reflect on a recent challenge you faced. How did you see God's presence during this time? How can you consider it pure joy despite the difficulties?

**One-sentence prayer:** Heavenly Father, thank you for my trials.

***Further hope and encouragement: James 1***

## DAY 31

# Turn Your Worries to Prayer

*Do not be anxious about anything, but in everything, by prayer
and petition, with thanksgiving, present your requests to God.
Philippians 4:6*

There is so much fear in the world today. You may be anxious at this very moment. Anxiety, worry, and fear can be crippling. I've been there many times. We are quick to think about the worst thing that could happen, preventing us from seeing the best that could happen. Life often comes with stress and anxiety, especially when faced with difficult decisions, uncertainty, relational conflict, or concerns about the well-being of those we care about. When we worry, we make ourselves bigger than Almighty God, as if we are the ones in control. Worry consumes our energy and clouds our ability to live with clarity and faith.

Here's the thing: God calls us to do what we cannot do on our own, but He will always provide everything we need to do it with His strength. He stretches us beyond what we can do alone so there is only one way to turn—to Him. We must turn every worry, fear, and anxiety over to God in prayer. We are called not to be anxious about anything but to pray about everything with a thankful heart (Philippians 4:6-7). When we surrender our worries to God, He replaces our fear with peace that surpasses understanding. So, today, write "Worry List" at the top of a piece of paper. List every worry that comes to mind. Then, cross off "Worry" at the top and replace it with "Prayer." Turn your worries into prayers today, trusting God to carry you and your burdens.

**Journal:** What worries or fears are weighing on your heart today? Write them down, and as you do, reflect on Philippians 4:6-7. How can you turn each worry into a prayer? Spend time surrendering your burdens to God, trusting Him to replace your anxiety with His peace. How might this practice impact your faith?

**One-sentence prayer:** Heavenly Father, I give my worries to You today.

*Further hope and encouragement: Philippians 4*

## DAY 32
# Meet People Where They Are

*I am the good shepherd, I know my sheep and my sheep know me.*
*John 10:14*

When my daughter was in fourth grade, she had a teacher named Mrs. Soroka who completely changed her outlook on school. Before the year began, there were days when even going to school felt like a struggle. But something shifted that year. Mornings that were once filled with reluctance were replaced by her doing cartwheels and toe touches in the kitchen. The difference? Mrs. Soroka took the time to truly know her. She understood my daughter's likes and dislikes, her strengths and growth areas, and most importantly, who she was as a person. My daughter noticed that, and when I would ask her what was different about the school year, she would say, "Mrs. Soroka understands me." This connection motivated her to always give her best, and now she dreams of becoming a fourth-grade teacher herself because of Mrs. Soroka's impact on her. The impact of being known and understood inspired her to believe in her potential and reach higher than she thought possible.

In John 10:14, Jesus says, "I am the good shepherd; I know my sheep and my sheep know me." God models for us what it means to meet people where they are. He knows us by name, understands our fears and hopes, and walks with us in every season of life. We are called to do the same. Whether in our homes, at work, in our churches, or wherever we may be—with our spouses, kids, friends, or anyone in our presence—we are called to take the time to truly know others—understanding their strengths, struggles, and stories. When we do, we build trust and inspire confidence. Like my daughter with Mrs. Soroka, we want those around us to say, "_____ understands me." It's then that we create a culture and environment in which people feel valued, motivated, and equipped to thrive. Keep meeting people where they are, following the example of our Good Shepherd, and watch how it transforms your relationships, life, and purpose.

**Journal:** Reflect on a time when someone truly understood you and how it impacted your sense of belonging and growth. How can you model that same understanding, as Jesus does for us, to the people in your life, ensuring they feel seen, valued, and supported in their journey?

**One-sentence prayer:** Heavenly Father, help me see and understand those around me, just as You see and know me.

*Further hope and encouragement: John 10:1-21*

## DAY 33
# Be Still

*Be still and know that I am God; I will be exalted among
the nations, I will be exalted in the earth.
Psalm 46:10*

I struggle to be still. I prefer to be on the move, accomplishing tasks and crossing off items on my to-do list. I am more anxious when I'm not working than when I'm at work. I prefer to be in the action and struggle to step away. Silence and stillness don't come naturally to me. A research study was conducted at Duke University (2014), often referred to as the "shocking study," in which participants were asked to spend time alone in a room with nothing but their thoughts. The only other items in the room were a chair and an electric shock apparatus. In the first experiment, 67% of participants chose to administer electric shocks to themselves rather than spend fifteen minutes alone in silence.

I would probably be guilty of being part of the percentage that chose to shock themselves. We must discipline ourselves to be still. As we create space in our day to be with God, we must allow our hearts and minds to be still. In our stillness, we quiet the world around us and trust God. As the psalmist says in Psalm 46:10, no matter what is happening around us, God is our refuge and strength, and He will be exalted. Our minds are too easily distracted and pulled elsewhere. Embracing stillness is a necessity; carve out dedicated moments in your day for quiet reflection, allowing God's presence to guide your thoughts and decisions. When you can't sleep? Be still. When you're doing your devotions? Be still. When the stresses of the day rise? Be still. In a culture that rushes from one thing to the next, allow yourself to be still and trust that God is in control.

**Journal:** Think about a moment today when you could choose to be still and invite God's presence into your heart. How can you create space in your day for quiet reflection, even in the midst of your busyness?

**One-sentence prayer:** Heavenly Father, help me to slow down and be still.

***Further hope and encouragement: Psalm 46***

# DAY 34
# The Work is Too Heavy for You

*You and these people who come to you will only wear yourselves out.*
*The work is too heavy for you; you cannot handle it alone.*
*Exodus 17:7*

There's a burnout culture in today's world. A culture of picking yourself up by the bootstraps and getting things done yourself. A culture of pushing through exhaustion and not asking for help. A culture of needing to work at all times to get ahead or not fall behind. I've been there too many times. As I look back at my journal entries, I often say, "I'm exhausted," "I'm struggling," and "I need rest." But guess what? I don't adjust and continue pushing through. I try to do too much on my own. From sunup to sundown, Moses was trying to lead the Israelites on his own. He was probably proud to show his father-in-law how hard he was working when his father-in-law told him, "What you are doing is not good" (Exodus 18:17). Moses was trying to be all things to all people, but even he couldn't carry the weight of responsibility alone.

Life is too heavy for us to carry alone. For most of us, "the way we are living is not good." Life isn't about proving how much we can handle; it's about embracing humility, recognizing our limited capacity, and involving others in the journey. It's also about relying on God's strength to guide us through the burdens we are called to carry. Let me ask you this: Is the way you're living sustainable? If not, it's time to pause, delegate, and trust others to walk alongside you. The weight of life is too much for one person—don't burn yourself out. Live with wisdom, share the load, and lean on God.

**Journal:** Is the way you're living sustainable? Write down areas where you feel overwhelmed or stretched too thin. Identify one task or responsibility you can delegate this week and who you can trust to help carry the load. What step will you take today to share the weight of life?

**One-sentence prayer:** Heavenly Father, I humbly recognize that I cannot walk this journey alone.

***Further hope and encouragement: Exodus 17***

# DAY 35
# Purpose in the Unknown

*And we know that in all things God works for the good of those*
*who love Him, who have been called according to His purpose.*
*Romans 8:28*

Purpose. It's something we wrestle with constantly. What's my purpose? Am I living it out? Should I be doing something different? Why did this happen? How does this fit into God's plan? I was on a trip with Hope International in the Dominican Republic when we visited a couple serving as pastors in a local church. Their home was small, built from concrete with bars over the windows. The streets outside were littered with garbage, and the only way inside was by stepping up on cinder blocks. Inside, the temperature was well over ninety degrees, with no air conditioning to offer relief. As we arrived, a young boy—barefoot and shirtless—greeted us with a shy smile and little hugs. The wife was blind and a child on our trip, full of innocent curiosity, asked through a translator, "When did you go blind?" A follow-up question came: "How has it changed your life?" Her answer is something I will never forget. "I don't know what the purpose is, but I know that God has a purpose for it. With God, there is always a purpose."

And then—she prayed over us. Ivelisse, the one living in poverty, the one who had lost her sight, the one with every reason to despair—she lifted us up in prayer. I stood there, sweating in the humidity, surrounded by the weight of poverty, and yet completely humbled by this woman's faith. She didn't need to understand *why*. She simply trusted *who*. So let me encourage you, just as Ivelisse encouraged us that day. Maybe life is going well for you right now, or maybe it's not. Maybe you're battling sickness, or someone close to you is. Maybe you've experienced deep loss. Perhaps you just lost a job or feel stuck, waiting for God to open doors that haven't budged. Maybe you're wrestling with a relationship, or you're in a season that feels endless. You might be crying out, "Why, God?" Here's the truth: We don't have to know the why when we know the Who. No matter what you're walking through, hold on to these words from Ivelisse: "You may not know what the purpose is, but know that God has a purpose for it. With God, there's always a purpose."

**Journal:** Like Ivelisse, you may be facing something in your life that you don't understand. Is there a situation where you're struggling to see God's purpose? Take a moment to reflect and write a prayer, asking God to help you surrender the need for answers and, like Ivelisse, trust that He is working for your good and HIs glory.

**One-sentence prayer:** Heavenly Father, even when I don't understand, help me trust that You have a purpose for it all.

*Further hope and encouragement: Jeremiah 29*

# DAY 36
# New Morning Mercies

*Because of the Lord's great love we are not consumed, for his compassions never fail. They are new every morning, great is your faithfulness.*
*Lamentations 3:22-23*

As the teacher walked out of school at the end of a difficult day with a student, she looked at me and said, "It doesn't change how I feel about them. Tomorrow is a new day." One of the most powerful, yet challenging, mindsets we can carry into life and leadership is the belief that every day offers a fresh start. However, it's often easy to become consumed by anxiety about the future or to dwell on the past. We carry burdens, conversations, and unresolved situations with us from day to day, allowing them to weigh us down and steal our attention from the present. These distractions can prevent us from treating people with the grace they deserve, as grudges and lingering offenses cloud our interactions. We label days as "bad" or "good" based on our experiences, but God's truth offers a better way.

God's mercies are new every morning, not because of anything we've done or could ever do. His mercy isn't earned. We serve a God who doesn't hold grudges but meets us where we are with compassion and grace. When Adam and Eve sinned in the Garden of Eden, they hid in shame, knowing they were exposed. Yet how did God respond? By His great compassion, He clothed them. The teacher's words echo this truth: just as God offers us fresh mercy each day, we are called to do the same for others. Because of His undeserved compassion toward us, we can extend grace to those we lead. As a child of God, you are equipped with the mercy and compassion needed to overflow into the lives of others. His mercies are new today—embrace them and extend them to the people in your life.

**Journal:** Reflect on a time when you received grace or compassion from someone. How did it impact your growth and mindset? How can you intentionally offer that same grace to those you lead today?

**One-sentence prayer:** Heavenly Father, Your mercies are new today and every day.

***Further hope and encouragement: Lamentations 3***

## DAY 37

# Speak Words that Heal

*Gracious words are a honeycomb, sweet to the soul
and healing to the bones.*
*Proverbs 16:24*

Raise your hand if you've ever lost sleep over something you said. My hand is in the air. Have you ever had to call, text, email, or visit someone to apologize for your words? Guilty again. Sure, there are moments I've regretted staying silent—but most of my regrets come from what *has* come out of my mouth. And too often, the person I'm talking about isn't even in the room. A good friend of mine emphasizes Proverbs 16:24 with his family and encourages them to live it out wherever they go: "Gracious words are like honeycomb, sweet to the soul and healing to the bones."

That's the call: to speak words that heal. Words matter—whether spoken behind closed doors or directly to someone's face, they carry immense weight. The old playground rhyme couldn't be more wrong: "Sticks and stones may break my bones, but words will never hurt me." Broken bones often heal in weeks or months, but the wounds caused by careless, discouraging, or unkind words can linger for years. In contrast, gracious words bring sweetness to the soul and healing to the heart. But that kind of speech doesn't come naturally; it's a discipline that requires intentionality and humility. Ultimately, the words we speak are an overflow of the heart. Each of us—no matter our role or title—has a daily choice: Will our words be sweet and healing, or sharp and harmful? Choose to use your words for good. Let's be people who speak life. Let's speak words that heal.

**Journal:** Reflect on a recent conversation where you had the choice to speak words that either healed or harmed. What drove your choice in that moment? How did your words affect the other person and your relationship? Identify one concrete step you can take this week to ensure your speech becomes a source of sweetness and healing.

**One-sentence prayer:** Heavenly Father, fill my mouth with gracious words today that bring healing and encouragement to every heart I encounter.

*Further hope and encouragement: Proverbs 16, Ephesians 4*

## DAY 38

# Step Out of the Boat

*"Come," he said. Then Peter got down out of the boat,*
*walked on water and came toward Jesus.*
*Matthew 14:31*

Is there a comfort zone holding you back? Are you afraid to take the first step? In Matthew 14, the disciples encounter Jesus walking on water. Initially frightened, they hear Him say, "Take courage, it is I" (Matthew 14:27). Peter responds, "If it's you, tell me to come to you on the water." Jesus simply says, "Come." Peter steps out of the boat—leaving behind the safety and security of what he knows—and onto the water, trusting in Jesus. His bold decision wasn't about his own abilities but was deeply rooted in his faith in Christ. Peter's step of faith reminds us that great things happen when we trust God and act in obedience to His calling.

In life, we're often faced with moments when we need to leave the comfort of the familiar and step into the unknown. The first step is rarely easy, but it's essential. What "boat" do you need to step out of to follow God's plan for your life? It might be pursuing a new opportunity, having a difficult conversation, or trusting Him during a season of uncertainty. Like Peter, our trust in Jesus must anchor us, enabling us to move forward even when the outcome is unclear. Life often requires courage and faith. Today, listen to Jesus's call, embrace the discomfort, and take that first step. Trust Him—He won't let you sink.

**Journal:** What "boat" are you clinging to that's holding you back from stepping into God's plan? Reflect on how fear or comfort has kept you from taking a bold step. What is one action you can take this week to trust God and step into the unknown?

**One-sentence prayer:** Heavenly Father, guide me outside my comfort zone, trusting You today.

***Further hope and encouragement: Matthew 14:22-32***

## DAY 39

# Fix Your Eyes on Jesus

*But when he saw the wind, he was afraid and, beginning to sink,...*
*Matthew 14:30*

Yesterday, we saw Peter step out of the boat, walking on water toward Jesus. Today, we see what happened next. In Matthew 14:30, Peter, initially full of faith, becomes aware of the strong wind around him. Fear takes hold, and he begins to sink. This verse serves as a powerful reminder of the importance of keeping our focus on Jesus, especially with life's distractions and challenges. Like Peter, we often start with bold faith but falter when we focus on the storms instead of the Savior. His cry for help, however, shows us where our focus should return—on Jesus, who immediately reaches out to catch him.

Let's take an honest look at ourselves today. How often are we like Peter? We set out with good intentions, but when the winds start to blow, we get distracted and take our eyes off Jesus. The "winds" can take many forms—criticism, obstacles, temptations, anxiety, or even our own doubts. These distractions creep in, pulling our focus away from the One who calls us to move forward with faith. Here's the thing: when we fear man, we become slaves to fear. But we're called to fear God and God alone—and to fear Him is to live for Him. That kind of reverent fear gives us the confidence to live boldly. Fear of the world, fear of others, and fear of everything around us often rob us of the peace and courage we need to press on, as we worry about what people think or what might go wrong. Today, let's intentionally fix our eyes on Jesus, the author and perfecter of our faith (Hebrews 12:2). Walk toward Him, knowing that even when the winds blow, He will steady your steps.

**Journal:** Reflect on a recent challenge that caused you to lose focus on Jesus. What distractions—like fear or pressure—pulled your attention away from Him? Write down one way you can fix your eyes on Him today and trust Him to guide you through life's challenges.

**One-sentence prayer:** Heavenly Father, if I fix my eyes on You, I can walk on water.

*Further hope and encouragement: Matthew 14:22-32*

# DAY 40
# Lord, Save Me

*But when he saw the wind, he was afraid, and beginning to sink,
cried out, "Lord, save me!" Immediately Jesus reached out his hand
and caught him. "You of little faith," he said. "Why did you doubt?"*
*Matthew 14:30-31*

I remember one summer when I was a teenage boy, I went flounder fishing with my grandparents off the coast of Cape May, New Jersey. We were about 22 miles offshore, and fishing wasn't going too well. I turned to my cousin and said, "Watch this." Without thinking, I jumped into the ocean without a life vest. As soon as I hit the water, I regretted it. I imagined sharks circling as I treaded water in the dark Atlantic Ocean. Big waves started to roll in, and at times, I could see the boat, but just as quickly, it would disappear from view. I swam toward the boat, panicking, but when I got close enough, they opened the fish door, and my grandfather, Pap-Pap, reached out his hand to pull me into the safety of the boat.

Even though what I did was foolish, my grandfather was there to catch me when I needed it. That memory reminds me of Peter's cry to Jesus as he began to sink. Peter stepped out in faith, but the storm caused him to take his eyes off Jesus. The moment he was overwhelmed, he cried out, "Lord, save me!" And just as Jesus reached out to catch him, my grandfather reached out to pull me to safety. Jesus is always there, ready to catch us when we start to sink under the weight of fear or uncertainty. Just like Pap-Pap didn't hesitate to rescue me (from the sharks), Jesus is right there, ready to lift us up when we cry out. Cry out to Jesus today with the words, "Lord, save me," and picture Him extending His hand to you. He's there, ready to lift you up, steady your steps, and lead you through whatever storm you're facing.

**Journal:** Think of a time when you felt overwhelmed. How did you respond? Reflect on Peter's cry for help when he began to sink. What would it look like for you to cry out to Jesus in those moments of struggle? Write a prayer asking God to help you trust in His strength and guidance, instead of relying on your own.

**One-sentence prayer:** Heavenly Father, I'm sinking, save me!

*Further hope and encouragement: Matthew 14:22-32*

## DAY 41

# Watch Out for the My's and I's

*He said, "Is not this great Babylon I have built as the royal residence,*
*by my mighty power and for the glory of my majesty?"*
*Daniel 4:30*

Today's verse serves as a warning for all of us. You may read this quote from King Nebuchadnezzar and think, "Wow, did he really say that? I would never say anything like that." But let's break down the words Nebuchadnezzar uses:

Is not this great Babylon which I have built
by my mighty power
For the glory of my majesty

Danger, danger, danger. When we see words like my and I, we know something is off in the heart. Here's the warning for us: we can be more like Nebuchadnezzar than we realize. It's easy to get caught up in building our own kingdom, seeking recognition, success, and praise, instead of seeking God's kingdom. We may even think we're building God's kingdom while, in reality, we're building our own in the pursuit of power, our wants, our desires, and human approval. Like King Nebuchadnezzar, the My's and I's can fill our hearts, minds, and mouths. Instead, we are called to be strong in the Lord and in His mighty power (Ephesians 6:10). Notice that the verse doesn't say, "Be strong in yourself and in your mighty power." The truth is, we don't have any mighty power on our own. So, let me ask you: Do you wake up each day surrendering to build God's kingdom? Or do you wake up striving to build your own? Let's keep an eye out for the My's and I's today.

**Journal:** Reflect on Nebuchadnezzar's words. Are there areas of your life where you're seeking glory for yourself instead of focusing on God's kingdom? Write a prayer asking God to shift your focus to His glory and help you serve with humility.

**One-sentence prayer:** Heavenly Father, help me keep my eyes on Your kingdom today.

***Further hope and encouragement: Daniel 4:28-37***

# DAY 42
# Because You Say So

*Simon answered, "Master, we've worked hard all night and haven't caught anything. But because you said so, I will let down my nets."*
*Luke 5:5*

This passage makes me smile because I can picture myself as Simon Peter. They had worked hard, fishing all night, and didn't catch anything. I'm sure they were ready to head in when Jesus told Simon Peter, "Put out into deep water, and let down the nets for a catch" (v.4). I love Simon Peter's response to Jesus. He had to be exhausted and kindly slips in that they've been fishing all night and caught zero fish, but he ends with this: "But because you say so, I will let down my nets" (v.5). When he let down the nets, they caught such a large number of fish that the net began to break (v.6).

Peter's response, "Because you say so," reflects humility and a willingness to surrender his own understanding in favor of Jesus' command. Despite his fishing expertise and the exhaustion from working all night, Peter chose to obey Jesus' instruction, even when it didn't make sense. In life, we often encounter moments when our efforts don't seem to pay off, or we feel overwhelmed by circumstances. Sometimes, we think we know what's best, but God might be leading us in a different direction. Being able to say, "Because you say so," requires humility, obedience, and faith that God's wisdom surpasses our own. Even when things don't make sense or when we feel exhausted, trusting His guidance can lead to blessings beyond what we could have imagined. Today, let's live with the words, "Because you say so, God." Even in the midst of confusion, weariness, or uncertainty, trusting in His direction can bring new opportunities and growth we never expected.

**Journal:** Think of a time when God's direction didn't align with your own understanding. How did you respond? Reflect on areas where you may need to trust His guidance more, even when it's hard. Is there a situation in your life where you need to surrender and simply say, "Because you said so"?

**One-sentence prayer:** Heavenly Father, because you say so I will

*Further hope and encouragement: Luke 5:1-11*

## DAY 43
# Today's the Day

*Teach us to number our days aright, that we may gain a heart of wisdom.*
*Psalm 90:12*

When it comes to eating better, I can't count how many times I've said, "I'll start tomorrow" or "Next week is the week!" I know it's important to stick with a diet, but I've been stuck on the "I'll start tomorrow" diet for far too long now. That same "I'll start tomorrow" mentality has played out in many areas of my life. Before I know it, weeks turn into months, then months into years, and the thing I planned to begin never starts at all. Time is precious, and Psalm 90:12 reminds us, "Teach us to number our days aright, that we may gain a heart of wisdom." The word aright is key—it means correctly or properly. God calls us to steward our time wisely, not to let it slip away in endless delays.

What has God called you to begin today that you've been putting off? Where are you wasting time on things of little or no value? How should you be spending your time to align with His purpose? The clock of life is always ticking. Legendary football coach Vince Lombardi is often credited with saying, "I never lost a game, I just ran out of time." In sports, the team that scores the most points, runs, or goals within the allotted time wins. But unlike sports, life doesn't offer timeouts where the clock stops. There's no reviewing past plays and adding time back. The seconds, minutes, and hours of each day are set—and they're constantly moving. That's why developing daily rhythms for God's kingdom is so important. Whether it's committing to prayer, spending time in Scripture, or intentionally serving others, small daily choices shape the life God calls us to live. Don't wait for the perfect moment or another tomorrow that may never come. The time to start is now. The clock won't stop, but you can choose today to use your time for what truly matters, God's kingdom. Today's the day.

**Journal:** What is one thing God has been prompting you to start that you keep putting off? How can you create a daily habit to grow in faith and use your time for His purpose? What distractions do you need to set aside to focus on what truly matters in God's kingdom?

**One-sentence prayer:** Heavenly Father, help me to use my time wisely for Your kingdom and start today.

***Further hope and encouragement: Psalm 90***

## DAY 44
# Call 911

*In the day of my trouble I will call to you, for you will answer me.*
*Psalm 86:7*

A few years ago, I headed to my grandmother's burn pile with my son to burn a few items. It was a Monday that I had off work, and I thought I would go do some "man things" with my son. We could have simply placed the items at the end of our driveway for the trash company to pick up, but no, I thought it would be best to burn them. The fire started beautifully as we proudly admired it together as father and son. Then, I noticed something. The fire began spreading outward beyond the burn pile toward the woods and two barns. Uh oh. I was about to set the entire area on fire. In an embarrassing attempt, I ran about one hundred yards to the house to fill a bucket of water to throw on the fire. Let me add this for imagery: I was also in a boot after having plantar fasciitis surgery. By the time I limped back, most of the water had splashed out, and I was left with just a few drops that barely made a dent in the fire— it was like trying to put out a bonfire with a teaspoon. I quickly realized there was nothing more I could do, so I called...Carly. She told me to hang up and dial 911.

I don't know if you've ever had to dial 911, but it's humbling. You come to the end of yourself and recognize you can't do it alone and need help. In life, when things get tough, where do you go, where do you run, who do you call? Like me, do you try to fix things on your own, or do you numb the pain with distractions? Is pride getting in the way of simply calling out to God, saying, "God, I need you. Help me. I can't do this on my own"? David's example in Psalm 86:7 shows us the importance of calling on God when trouble strikes: "In the day of my trouble, I will call to you, for you will answer me." As much as I didn't want to call 911, you know what felt the best? Hearing the fire truck sirens approaching, knowing they were right there to help me. Today, remember that you don't have to face challenges alone. Call on your Heavenly Father, and He will answer you.

**Journal:** Think about a recent challenge where you tried to fix things on your own. How did that impact you, and what was the outcome? Reflect on how you can follow David's example in Psalm 86:7 by calling on God for wisdom and guidance when facing difficulties.

**One-sentence prayer:** Heavenly Father, I call upon You today.

***Further hope and encouragement: Psalm 86***

# DAY 45
# I Must Become Less

*He must become greater; I must become less.*
*John 3:30*

Today's verse spoken by John the Baptist is humbling and powerful. This world will tell us to go for more, more, more—keep striving to become greater and more well-known. A world of social media searching for more followers and more influence. But the Word tells us a different story—for Jesus to become greater, we must become less. John the Baptist was highly influential, and many people believed he might be the long-awaited Savior. But John clarified his role, letting people know that he was preparing the way for someone greater who would come after him (John 1:23).

In life, we must follow John's example of embracing genuine humility, acknowledging our limitations, and directing attention to Jesus rather than ourselves. We are called to live in a way that makes Jesus greater and us less. When we choose to decrease so that Christ may increase, we reflect the truth of Philippians 2:3: "Do nothing out of selfish ambition or conceit, but in humility consider others better than yourselves." When we make Jesus more important, we naturally shift our focus to serving and loving others rather than seeking recognition for ourselves. This kind of humility leaves a lasting impact far beyond anything we could accomplish on our own. In a world striving for more, begin today by humbly saying, "I must become less."

**Journal:** Where in your life do you find yourself striving for more—whether it's recognition, influence, success, or comfort and ease? How can embracing humility and focusing on making Jesus greater shift your perspective? Write about ways you can "become less" today, pointing others to Christ instead of seeking personal gain.

**One-sentence prayer:** Heavenly Father, I must become less—help me make You more.

***Further hope and encouragement: John 3:22-36***

# DAY 46
# Hiding Place

*You are my hiding place; you will protect me from*
*trouble and surround me with songs of deliverance.*
*Psalm 32:7*

Growing up, my cousin Matt and I spent our summers playing baseball, basketball, climbing trees, and drinking slushies. One morning, we decided to shoot hoops in the driveway. My mom's blue Ford Aerostar minivan was parked right beside the hoop, but instead of asking her to move it, we did what any kids would do—we played anyway. One of Matt's first shots hit the rim, bounced off, and smacked the windshield and a large crack suddenly appeared. It was the kind of crack that made you freeze in place, eyes wide as you slowly look at the person next to you, already planning your escape route before an adult could see the damage. That's exactly what my cousin did—he took off running and hid. I went inside to tell my mom what had happened (I guess you could call me a tattletale), and she came outside to help look for him. Eventually, we found him crouched in the bushes along the side of the house. He was bracing for the worst, expecting to get in trouble. But instead of scolding him, my mom wrapped him in a hug and said, "Everything is OK."

In Psalm 32, David says to God, "You are my hiding place; you will protect me from trouble" (v. 7). Unlike Adam and Eve, who tried to hide from God in the Garden of Eden, or my cousin, who hid out of fear, David understood that God Himself is our hiding place. There is no safer refuge than His presence. When we fall short—when we "mess up"—our instinct is often to run and hide. We avoid God when, in reality, He is the very one we need to run to. Just like my mom embraced my cousin with grace and compassion, God meets us in our failures with love, not condemnation. In our relationships, whether with family, friends, or coworkers, we have the opportunity to extend that same grace. When we create an environment where others feel safe owning their mistakes, we build trust, strengthen connections, and remind one another that growth often comes through our missteps. Turn to God today, He is your hiding place.

**Journal:** Think of a time when you or someone else made a mistake. How did you respond? Did it build trust or create fear? How can running to God as your hiding place help you extend grace to others?

**One-sentence prayer:** Heavenly Father, You are my hiding place.

***Further hope and encouragement: 1 Samuel 23, Psalm 31***

## DAY 47
# It is Written

*Jesus answered, "It is written: Man does not live on bread alone,*
*but on every word that comes from the mouth of God."*
*Matthew 4:4*

How do you react to difficulties in your life? How about worries and fears? Temptations? How do you respond when you achieve success or experience failure? There's no better model to follow than Jesus. I love how Jesus responds to Satan in the desert when being tempted after fasting for 40 days and 40 nights. Three times Jesus responded to the temptations with, "It is written," followed by quoting the Word of God.

We must do the same. Every moment of every day we must say, "It is written." But to say that, "It is written," we must know what is written. We must be in the Bible daily memorizing Scripture as we prepare for whatever comes our way.

+ When you're anxious…*It is written*: cast all your anxieties on him, because he cares for you (1 Peter 5:7).
+ When you're fearful…*It is written*: he said, "I will never leave or forsake you" (Hebrews 13:5)
+ When you're exhausted…*It is written*: He gives power to the faint, and to him who has no might he increases strength (Isaiah 40:29)
+ When you're frustrated with someone…*It is written*: A gentle answer turns away wrath, but a harsh word stirs up anger (Proverbs 15:1)
+ When you're tempted to speak poorly about someone…*It is written*: Do not let any unwholesome talk come out of your mouth, but only what is helpful for building others up according to their needs, that it may benefit those who listen (Ephesians 4:32).

And remember, to say, "It is written," we must know what is written.

**Journal:** Identify one specific area where you struggle—whether it's sin, anxiety, frustration, or exhaustion—and find a verse to memorize this week. How can embedding God's Word in your heart prepare you to respond with wisdom and grace in the future?

**One-sentence prayer:** Heavenly Father, it is written

_____.

*Further hope and encouragement: Matthew 4:1-11*

# DAY 48
# Stronger Together

*If one falls down, his friend can help him up.*
*Ecclesiastes 4:10*

I often jammed my fingers while playing basketball growing up. I vividly remember the feeling of the basketball hitting my finger at just the wrong spot, sending a sharp pain through my hand. For days or even weeks, my finger would be sore, making it difficult to bend. To keep playing, the athletic trainer would "buddy tape" the injured finger to a healthy one. If I jammed my pointer finger, my middle finger would be wrapped alongside it, providing support and stability. The injured finger was too weak on its own, but with extra reinforcement, I could keep playing and performing at a higher level.

Life works the same way. We aren't meant to go through it alone. At times, we all feel weak, overwhelmed, or unsure of how to move forward. But when we have the right people around us—friends, family, and a church community—we find strength beyond what we could do on our own. As the Teacher reminds us in *Ecclesiastes 4:10*, "*If one falls down, his friend can help him up.*" Who is your "buddy tape" in life? Who supports you when you're struggling, encourages you when you're discouraged, and helps you keep going? Just as my injured finger needed reinforcement, we all need people who come alongside us, offering strength and stability. We are stronger when we face life together.

**Journal:** Who is your "buddy tape" in life—someone who strengthens and supports you? Reflect on an area where you've been carrying the weight alone. How can inviting others to walk alongside you bring encouragement and stability?

**One-sentence prayer:** Heavenly Father, I'm weak and vulnerable on my own, I can't do it alone.

**Further hope and encouragement: Ecclesiastes 4:7-12**

## DAY 49
# Delight in Difficulties

*That is why for Christ's sake, I delight in weaknesses, in insults, in hardships,*
*in persecutions, in difficulties. For when I am weak, then I am strong.*
*2 Corinthians 12:10*

You've probably heard people encourage gratitude walks or starting each day by listing things you're thankful for—health, family, recent successes, the sunrise, the sunset, or shelter, just to name a few. While there's certainly nothing wrong with focusing on the positive, I want to challenge you to shift your perspective for a moment. We often spend so much time looking for the good and celebrating the blessings in our lives, which is important, but there's another side to the story—one that invites us to look at our struggles and difficulties in a different light.

Today, Instead of simply focusing on the good things, take a moment to reflect on the hardships and difficulties in your life. But don't stop there—delight in them. Whether it's something you're experiencing now or something from your past, think of the moments when you felt weakest and had no idea what God was doing. Don't fall into self-pity, but instead reflect on how God used, or is using, those seasons of weakness to strengthen you for your good and His glory. For me, I think of a season of deep depression and anxiety or a battle with asthma and low oxygen that kept me in and out of the hospital for nearly a year. During that time, I had no clear answers, but now I see how God used it to soften and shape my heart. As you reflect, remember the hardship Jesus endured on the cross for you and me—offering us eternal hope. Delight in your difficulties today, trusting that God is working through them.

**Journal:** Think of a difficulty God has used to strengthen you. How has it shaped you? Delight in that difficulty.

**One-sentence prayer:** Heavenly Father, I delight in the difficulties of life today.

***Further hope and encouragement: 2 Corinthians 12***

# DAY 50
# Less Striving, More Abiding

*"Martha, Martha," the Lord answered, "you are worried and upset about many things, but only one thing is needed. Mary has chosen what is better, and it will not be taken away from her."*
*Luke 10: 41-42*

Burnout is a common feeling many people find themselves experiencing today. We often get caught up in the busyness of life—working, running errands, managing relationships, and taking care of everything that needs attention. We pour ourselves into countless tasks, striving to succeed, but often end up feeling anxious, drained, and overwhelmed. Time off may offer temporary relief, but if we don't adjust how we approach our lives, that burnout cycle will continue.

The story of Mary and Martha in Luke 10:38-42 illustrates this perfectly. Martha was consumed by the tasks at hand, trying to make everything perfect, while Mary chose to sit at Jesus' feet, listening to Him and resting in His presence. Jesus gently reminded Martha that Mary had chosen the better path—being still and abiding with Him. In our own lives, it's easy to become like Martha—preoccupied with our never-ending to-do lists and constantly striving to do more, even when we set out with the intention of doing good. We often find ourselves "worried and upset about many things," forgetting to take time to sit at the feet of Jesus. When we place our identity in what we do—our jobs, roles, and achievements—rather than in Christ, burnout becomes inevitable. But when we remember who we are and Whose we are, it transforms how we live. We shift from living a life of *striving* to living a life of *abiding*, resting in His grace and peace.

**Journal:** Reflect on your life: Are you more like Martha, striving and anxious, or Mary, resting in God's presence? What's one way you can focus more on abiding in Jesus this week?

**One-sentence prayer:** Heavenly Father, I want to strive less and abide in You more today.

***Further hope and encouragement: Luke 10:38-42***

# DAY 51
# Rest, Think, Trust

*In repentance and rest is your salvation, in quietness and*
*trust is your strength, but you would have none of it.*
*Isaiah 30:15*

In life, we're constantly moving from one thing to another, rarely stopping long enough to think. That quote was repeated over and over again in my principal courses. Yet here I am—a principal, father, husband, coach, and elder—always doing something. I move from one task to the next, one meeting to another, one event to the next. In between, I can often be found staring at my phone, mindlessly scrolling through social media or checking sports updates and breaking news. If I'm being honest, I avoid quietness and stillness. I'm convicted when my kids constantly seek entertainment, and I tell them, "You need to learn to be bored." The truth is, I avoid boredom myself. I steer clear of those moments when I feel more deeply or think more intentionally. Whether consciously or not, I've developed a habit of busyness and struggle with downtime. If we're being honest, we don't want to allow boredom. We don't want to be alone with our thoughts. We don't want to think and feel. We just want to hide it all in busyness. But eventually, it catches up with us.

Then, there are moments when it all catches up with me—when I feel overwhelmed and think, I can't do it all anymore. That's when I realize I've lost the rhythm God designed for our lives. In creation, God worked for six days, and on the seventh day, He rested. God didn't need to rest, but He modeled how we should live. I love driving past a closed Chick-fil-A on Sundays. Why? Because it's a powerful reminder that we will be just fine when we take time to rest. In fact, we'll be better for it. The following three words may be hard to hear—I know they are for me—but we must rest. We must allow boredom. We must think, feel, and reflect—on our faith in Jesus, our work, and our lives. Step out of the relentless cycle of busyness. Plan a day in the near future to put your phone away, take a walk outside, journal, or set aside twenty-four hours when you don't try to advance yourself. Simply pause. Rest. Think. Trust.

**Journal:** When was the last time you truly allowed yourself to be still? What happened in that moment? How can you create more intentional space for rest and reflection in your daily life?

**One-sentence prayer:** Heavenly Father, help me embrace rest, stillness, and reflection to better align with You.

*Further hope and encouragement: Isaiah 30*

# DAY 52
# Practicing the Pause

*Blessed are the peacemakers, for they will be called children of God.*
*Matthew 5:9*

One afternoon, I received an email from my superintendent's office asking me to call an upset father. He had bypassed me and taken his concerns straight to the top. Frustrated by the situation, I made a mistake that I like to think is not typical of me: I called him immediately. My frustration spilled into the conversation, and within minutes, we were going back and forth with one another, neither truly listening. Suddenly, I realized I was only escalating the conflict. I paused, took a breath, and said, "I'm sorry. Can I please start this conversation over?" That moment shifted the tone entirely. We were able to talk, listen, and ultimately resolve the issue.

In life, we are called to be peacemakers, reflecting Jesus, the Prince of Peace. Isaiah 9:6 declares, "For to us a child is born... And he will be called Wonderful Counselor, Mighty God, Everlasting Father, Prince of Peace." To live as He did, we must prioritize peace, even when our emotions are stirred. Sometimes, this means practicing the pause—choosing not to respond immediately when we're feeling frustrated or upset. Instead, we reflect, pray, and respond with wisdom and grace. Life provides countless opportunities to be a peacemaker, whether it's defusing a tense situation with a friend or loved one, resolving misunderstandings, or showing kindness in difficult conversations. Today, focus on being a peacemaker by choosing words and actions that point people to Jesus.

**Journal:** Reflect on a recent moment when you had the opportunity to practice the pause. How did you respond, and what might you do differently next time to bring peace to the situation?

**One-sentence prayer:** Heavenly Father, help me to reflect Your peace today.

***Further hope and encouragement: Matthew 5:1-11***

# DAY 53
# Daily Bread

*Give us this day our daily bread.*
*Matthew 6:11*

Too often, we fail to trust God in the moment and instead wait for the "perfect" moment. I'll cut to the chase—there is no "perfect" moment. Sometimes we simply need to step outside our comfort zone before we feel ready. We need to step out of our doubts and into our faith. Paul Tripp (2014) says, "You don't try to figure out what God is going to do next and how he will meet your needs; you move forward in the certainty that He is with you, for you, and in you. This God of awesome power will grant you power to do what is needed." You may have woken up feeling weak. God is not. You may have woken up feeling vulnerable. God is not. You may have woken up feeling unprepared. God is not. When you feel ill-equipped for what lies ahead, God is not.

God has promised to supply you with what you need for each day. Trust Him. He is your daily bread. When Jesus taught the disciples to pray the Lord's Prayer, He said, "Give us this day our daily bread" (Matthew 6:11). God is the one who will provide you with what you need for each day. Life is about following God and trusting Him every step of the way. Don't let fear and uncertainty hold you back from embracing the opportunities and blessings He has placed before you. Faith isn't about having all the answers or feeling perfectly prepared. It's about faithfully stepping forward, trusting that God has already equipped you with everything you need for today. Lean into His strength, and remember that your limitations are opportunities for His grace to shine through. Don't worry about tomorrow—ask God to provide your daily bread today. He is with you, for you, and in you.

**Journal:** How often do you wait for the "perfect" moment? Reflect on a current challenge or decision where you feel unprepared or uncertain. How can you step forward in faith, trusting that God has already equipped you with what you need for today?

**One-sentence prayer:** Heavenly Father, fill me with Your daily bread.

***Further hope and encouragement: Matthew 6:5-15***

# DAY 54
# Word of Mouth

*In everything set them an example by doing what is good. In your
teaching show integrity, seriousness, and soundness of speech that
cannot be condemned, so that those who oppose you may be
ashamed because they have nothing bad to say about us.*
*Titus 2:7-8*

I met Miguel in the Dominican Republic. Miguel is gifted with his hands, building small projects like kitchen cabinets for his small business. He even demonstrated his skills for us. When we asked him how he gained work and clients, he explained, through a translator, "Word of mouth." He told us that when he does good work, people tell others about it, and those referrals help his small business grow. Miguel shared that his greatest satisfaction comes not just from completing a project, but from knowing his work speaks for itself, bringing in good referrals. As he described it, "My greatest satisfaction is a job well done and good referrals."

The truth is, our lives should be the same way. We are not called to live for human praise, but we are called to live in such a way that when people see us, they can't help but see God's goodness through us. Just as Miguel's work led to referrals, our lives should serve as a "referral" to others—a living testimony of God's grace and love. Titus 2:7-8 encourages us to live out integrity and goodness so that others have nothing bad to say about us—just like when someone is asked about Miguel's work, the only answer is, "It's excellent, and I highly recommend him." Here's a thought: If someone were to look at your life, could they say, "_____ referred me to you, Jesus, by the way they live their life"? Does your life reflect Jesus so clearly that people are drawn to know Him? Whether in word or action, whether people are watching or not, like Miguel's work, let your life be a testimony that speaks volumes, not just about you, but about your Heavenly Father.

**Journal:** Think about the way you live your life—whether at work, at home, or in your community. How do your actions and words reflect your faith in Jesus? Write about specific ways you can live as a "referral" to others, pointing them to Christ through your life.

**One-sentence prayer:** Heavenly Father, help me live in such a way that my life reflects Your goodness, and others are drawn to You through my actions and words.

*Further hope and encouragement: Matthew 5:13-16*

## DAY 55

# This is the Day the Lord Has Made

*This is the day the Lord has made, we will rejoice and be glad in it.*
*Psalm 118:24*

Inky Johnson is a former college football player and a highly regarded motivational speaker. His story is one of faith, perseverance, and overcoming adversity. Johnson played cornerback for the University of Tennessee and was on track for a promising NFL career. However, in 2006, during a routine play, he suffered a life-altering injury that left his right arm permanently paralyzed. Instead of letting his injury define him, Johnson uses his experience to inspire others. Every day, he tweets out the same verse: "This is the day the Lord has made; so let us rejoice and be glad in it" (Psalm 118:24).

What an incredible mindset to take into each day—knowing that no matter what happens, God is sovereign, and His plans for us remain good.

+ When you get a harsh email or phone call—*This is the day the Lord has made...*
+ When you don't get the job you were hoping for—*This is the day the Lord has made...*
+ When nothing seems to be going your way—*This is the day the Lord has made...*
+ When everything seems to be falling into place—*This is the day the Lord has made...*
+ When you feel like giving up—*This is the day the Lord has made...*

Each day is a gift from God, no matter what it holds. Just as the Psalmist and Inky Johnson choose to rejoice daily, we, too, have the choice to anchor our hearts in this truth. We are not defined by our circumstances but by our trust in God's plan. So go out with confidence today, knowing that this is the day the Lord has made.

**Journal:** What challenges or joys are you facing today? How can you adopt the mindset that "This is the day the Lord has made"? In what ways can you choose to rejoice, regardless of your circumstances?

**One-sentence prayer:** Heavenly Father, no matter what today holds, help me rejoice and trust that this is the day You have made.

*Further hope and encouragement: Psalm 118*

## DAY 56

# Pray Like Daniel

*Now when Daniel learned that the decree had been published,
he went home to his upstairs room where the windows opened toward
Jerusalem. Three times a day he got down on his knees and prayed,
giving thanks to his God, just as he had done before.*
*Daniel 6:10*

There was a season in my principal journey when finding support staff members felt impossible. The lack of personnel was affecting the culture and climate of our school—teachers were stretched thin, and we struggled to meet our students' needs. Frustration began to creep in as I brainstormed, networked, and even advertised in ways I hadn't before. During a conversation with a mentor, I vented about the challenges of finding quality support staff. He listened and then gently asked, *"Well, have you prayed about it?"* His question stopped me in my tracks. I hadn't. I felt convicted as he encouraged me to pray over everything, even something like staffing. He reminded me that no detail is too small—or too big—for God. That moment shifted my perspective. I began bringing the staffing needs before God daily, trusting Him to open the right doors.

Daniel was a man of prayer, no matter the circumstance. When things were going well, he prayed. When challenges arose, he prayed. When he needed wisdom and guidance, he prayed. And when he was told not to, he prayed. Daniel 6:10 tells us that "three times a day he got down on his knees and prayed, giving thanks to his God, just as he had done before." Even under the threat of the lion's den, Daniel remained steadfast in prayer. He trusted God's sovereignty and sought Him consistently, modeling what it looks like to depend on God in all things. Whatever you're facing today—whether it's a difficult decision, an unexpected challenge, something that seems too small and simple, or something heavy on your heart—bring it before God in prayer. Trust His timing and His provision, and watch how He moves in ways you never expected.

**Journal:** What is one situation you've been giving a lot of attention to and trying really hard to figure out, but haven't stopped to pray about? How can you surrender it to God today?

**One-sentence prayer:** Heavenly Father, help me turn to You in every situation, trusting that no detail of my life is too small or too big for Your hands.

*Further hope and encouragement: Daniel 6*

# DAY 57
# Withdraw

*But Jesus often withdrew to lonely places and prayed.*
*Luke 5:16*

I'm the type of person who waits until my car's gas gauge is almost empty before I stop for gas. I love driving fast down the highway, I have places to be, people to see, and there is no time for pulling off at the exits! But guess what? I'm also the type of person who gets extremely anxious when my gas tank is low fearing that I'll run out of gas. Those two traits don't go well together. I don't like to slow down or stop and I push myself to exhaustion until I finally try to stop and refuel myself. Other times I'll continue pushing through my exhaustion. Much like when I'm driving and running low on gas, I become anxious, worried, and irritable until I make the time to stop and refuel. The same is true in life—running on empty and anxiety often go hand in hand.

Jesus modeled the perfect way to withdraw and refuel by purposefully stepping aside to spend time with his Heavenly Father. People wanted to be around Jesus, talk to Jesus, listen to Jesus, and be healed by Jesus. He made it a priority in his life to withdraw to lonely places where he prayed (Luke 5:16). In life, we can't be running on empty all the time. Refueling isn't optional; it's essential. So how about you today? Are you speeding down the highway of life, needing to pull over to a rest stop to refuel but pushing through anyway? Do you see the rest stops but keep driving past them? Or do you feel like there are no rest stops in sight? Where's your gas tank today? When we make time to rest, reflect, and spend time with God, we not only restore our energy but also gain clarity and strength to live with greater peace, wisdom, and discernment. Make it a habit to withdraw.

**Journal:** Reflect on your current pace. Are you running on empty, anxious and worn out? How can you intentionally withdraw and refuel in order to live with renewed strength, clarity, and wisdom? Consider setting aside time each day for rest, reflection, and prayer to restore your energy and sharpen your focus.

**One-sentence prayer:** Heavenly Father, help me refuel in You today.

*Further hope and encouragement: Psalm 42:1-2, Psalm 61:1-2*

# DAY 58
# Good Samaritan

*But a Samaritan, as he traveled, came where the man was;*
*and when he saw him, he took pity on him.*
*Luke 10:33*

In life, it can be tempting to hide from difficult situations or avoid certain people, hoping the problem will resolve itself. We might even change our path or routine to steer clear of uncomfortable conversations or conflicts. When I was serving as an assistant principal, my principal taught me a valuable lesson: "Run to the fire." He explained that we can never run away from an issue; instead, we must move toward it. Whether it be a strained relationship, a difficult conversation, a personal challenge, or someone in need—we must go toward it.

The parable of the Good Samaritan teaches us a valuable life lesson. A man had been beaten, robbed, and left on the side of the street. A priest and Levite walked by, saw the need, and crossed to the other side of the road to avoid the man. But when the Samaritan walked by, he saw him and went to him. Just as the Good Samaritan didn't avoid the man in need but went directly to him, we must take the same approach in life—running to the "fire" and addressing the situation with compassion and courage. This requires both the bravery to confront difficult situations and the heart to care deeply for the people involved. Be someone who doesn't shy away from the tough moments, but steps into them with integrity and a willingness to serve. Be a Good Samaritan today and run to the fire.

**Journal:** Think about a difficult situation or conversation you're avoiding. How can you approach it with the same courage and compassion as the Good Samaritan? Reflect on ways you can "run to the fire" today, stepping into challenges with integrity and a heart to serve.

**One-sentence prayer:** Heavenly Father, give me eyes to see the needs of others and be a Good Samaritan today.

***Further hope and encouragement: Luke 10:25-37***

# DAY 59
# Haven't You Read?

*"Haven't you read?" he replied.*
*Matthew 19:4*

Where do you look for answers when you have a question? If you're struggling with conflict, where do you turn? What about worry or fear? Where do you go when you're losing the joy you once had? What do you watch, listen to, or turn to for wisdom and discernment? When you're exhausted, where does your strength come from? What guides you through your life? Is it a podcast, a self-help book, Google, or artificial intelligence? Look no further than the bare Word of God. One of the main reasons I began writing was that I found everything I was learning had already been written in the Bible. While many books inform, the Bible transforms.

We previously looked at Jesus responding to temptation with, "It is written," followed by reciting Scripture. If you're searching for answers to your daily circumstances, let me ask you the same three words that Jesus asked: "Haven't you read?" (Matthew 19:4). Jesus often questioned people's understanding of the Scriptures with these words. As Paul says in 2 Timothy 3:16, "All Scripture is God-breathed and is useful for teaching, rebuking, correcting, and training in righteousness, so that the servant of God may be thoroughly equipped for every good work." We often search for quick fixes and magic formulas, but the answer is right there in the bare Word of God. Just as Scripture equips us for righteousness, it also equips us for the daily decisions we face—decisions that require not just knowledge, but discernment. So, let me close with the same question Jesus asks: "Haven't you read?"

**Journal:** Think about a recent challenge or decision you faced. How did you seek guidance, and how might God's Word offer wisdom for that situation? What steps can you take today to make reading Scripture a regular part of your life?

**One-sentence prayer:** Heavenly Father, help me to make space to read Your Word.

*Further hope and encouragement: Matthew 12:3-5, Matthew 21:16, Psalm 119:9-16*

# DAY 60
# Work for the Glory of God

*So whether you eat drink or whatever you do,*
*do it all for the glory of God.*
*1 Corinthians 10:31*

One of my favorite things to do around the house is mow the lawn. Let me be clear that I have a riding mower and I enjoy hopping on and cutting the grass. It doesn't take much effort. Here's a little secret: when I get to the trampoline in our backyard, I usually mow around it. Guess what? Carly can't stand that I don't take the time to get off the mower, move the trampoline, and mow underneath where the trampoline was standing. In my defense, I do move the trampoline and mow it about every other week (OK, every third week). However, the grass typically stands a few inches taller underneath the trampoline. She tells me point blank, "That's lazy. Don't cut corners."

Paul says in 1 Corinthians, "So whether you eat or drink or whatever you do, do it all for the glory of God" (v. 31). Let's be honest: we all face the temptation to cut corners in life. When we cut corners, we fall short of doing everything for God's glory. Sometimes we may do just enough so that others see us completing tasks, whether it's at work, at home, or in our relationships. However, that's not what God calls us to do. He doesn't call us to do just enough to get by or a job that's "good enough." People notice when we prioritize excellence and integrity in our daily tasks and work. God calls us to do everything for His glory. So, don't cut corners today. Work for the Glory of God.

**Journal:** Think about an area of your life where you may have been tempted to cut corners. How can you bring greater excellence to that area today? What steps can you take to ensure your work, your relationships, and your daily tasks are done for God's glory, not just to meet expectations?

**One-sentence prayer:** Heavenly Father, I'm working for Your glory today.

*Further hope and encouragement: 1 Corinthians 10:23-33*

## DAY 61
# Surrender

*I am the vine, you are the branches. If a man remains in me and I in him,*
*he will bear much fruit, apart from me you can do nothing.*
*John 15:5*

If you're like me, you spend your days striving. Most mornings, I wake up with the fear of falling behind if I don't push ahead. The definition of strive is to make great efforts to achieve or obtain something. Does that sound like you? It can certainly be a good thing, but unfortunately, we often strive after the wrong things. In life, we're tempted to measure success by our accomplishments and efforts. Today, instead of striving, let's focus on surrender.

John 15:5 is one of my favorite verses, where Jesus says, "apart from me, you can do nothing" (John 15:5). But if we remain in Jesus and He in us, we can bear fruit. If you're at home, in your office, or wherever you are, get on your knees in prayer and surrender to Jesus, humbly saying, "Apart from You, I can do nothing."

+ Surrender that you can't breathe without Him.
+ Surrender that you can't stand without Him.
+ Surrender that you can't walk or talk without Him.
+ Surrender that God is in control of everything, and you're not.
+ Surrender that difficult conversation you have today.
+ Surrender your exhaustion.
+ Surrender your anxieties, fears, and worries.
+ Surrender your struggles and doubts.
+ And last, but not least, surrender your striving.

Surrender, surrender, surrender. Surrender it all this morning and every morning. When we surrender, we move from striving for control to living with purpose, letting God guide our daily decisions, conversations, and actions. Humbly confess that life is too heavy on our own, but through Jesus, we can bear much fruit. Apart from Him, we can do nothing.

**Journal:** Reflect on an area of your life where you've been striving or trying to control the outcome. How can you surrender that to God today, trusting that He is the source of your strength?

**One-sentence prayer:** Heavenly Father, help me to surrender to You today and trust that You are in control.

***Further hope and encouragement: John 15:1-16***

## DAY 62
# Work/Life Rhythm

*God saw all that he had made, and it was very good.*
*And there was evening, and there was morning—the sixth day.*
*Genesis 1:31*

There's no such thing as a work/life balance. Yet, we hear it over and over again when discussing self-care: "How is your work/life balance?" Picture a teeter-totter—or you may know it as a seesaw. Wow. Do you remember those on playgrounds? One person sits on one side, and another sits on the other. Now, think about how a teeter-totter works. You try to find someone of a similar size and weight—it doesn't have to be exact. Then, one person uses their feet to push off the ground, rising into the air while the other person lowers to the ground. That person then pushes off, sending themselves up while the other goes down. This rhythm continues as both people move up and down, smiling at one another.

Here's the thing: a teeter-totter is designed to move rhythmically, not to be perfectly equal. Imagine a scale in science class—if the two sides were exactly balanced, both people would be stuck in midair, feet dangling, staring awkwardly at one another. And if the weight is too unevenly distributed, someone will get stuck on the ground or suspended in the air. Don't let yourself get stuck. More than ever, work follows you home, and home follows you to work. You're never going to find perfect balance. Instead, you need to find a rhythm that works for you and your family. And don't compare yourself to others—how long someone stays at work or how clean someone's house is. Everyone's rhythm is different, and it changes with the season. Quit striving for balance—you'll never get there. Instead, rest in the truth that some seasons of life, the year, or even the week will be more demanding than others. Some days, you'll get to work on time and leave on time. Other times, you'll need to head in early or stay a little later. Find your rhythm. And trust that it's enough.

**Journal:** Just as God created the world with rhythm and purpose, how can you embrace the rhythms in your own life? How can you adjust your rhythm to align with what matters most right now—without guilt or comparison?

**One-sentence prayer:** Heavenly Father, help me embrace the rhythm You have set for my life, trusting that each season has a purpose in Your greater plan.

***Further hope and encouragement: Genesis 1***

# DAY 63
# Struggling to Communicate

*Therefore, as God's chosen people, holy and dearly loved, clothe yourselves with compassion, kindness, humility, gentleness, and patience.*
*Colossians 3:12*

It was my first time raising a teenager—well, almost a teenager. My oldest daughter, Olivia, was 12 and approaching her 13th birthday. I often joke that I'm not ready to be a parent. Parenting is hard! I could sense some distance developing between Livi and me. It wasn't that things were bad, but something felt "off." As a twelve-year-old girl, she was struggling to communicate, and as a first-time dad of an almost-teenage daughter, I was struggling, too. One morning, as she was getting ready for school, I walked up to her, put my arm around her, and she put one arm around me. I said, "Livi, I want you to know that I love you. I don't always know what to say or do, but I want you to know I'm always right here by your side."

Communication can make or break a relationship—it can build trust, or it can destroy it. As Peter Drucker (1967) once said, "The most important thing in communication is hearing what isn't said." Colossians 3:12 reminds us, "Therefore, as God's chosen people, holy and dearly loved, clothe yourselves with compassion, kindness, humility, gentleness, and patience." The way we speak—or don't speak—has the power to heal or hurt. So, how about you? Take some time to reflect on your relationships—with your spouse, kids, coworkers, parents, friends, you name it. Is there a relationship that needs your attention today? Maybe, like me, you sense a struggle but don't know what to say. Start by simply letting them know they matter to you. You don't need perfect words—just the reassurance that you are there by their side. Let's clothe ourselves today with compassion, kindness, humility, gentleness, and patience today – especially in the moments when communication feels hardest.

**Journal:** Is there someone in your life with whom communication feels strained? Have your words been building them up or creating distance? What is one simple way you can show them you are there for them today? Remember, it may not even include many words.

**One-sentence prayer:** Heavenly Father, help me to listen with love, speak with wisdom, and always communicate in a way that builds others up.

***Further hope and encouragement: Colossians 3***

# DAY 64
# From Shepherds to Sheep

*But first, seek his kingdom and his righteousness,*
*and all these things will be given to you as well.*
Matthew 6:33

Jesus was born in a humble manger. The first to hear of this incredible news were not royalty but lowly shepherds, who were out in the fields tending to their flocks at night. As the angel announced, "Do not be afraid; I bring you good news that will cause great joy for all the people," the shepherds were called to stop what they were doing and search for the Savior. They lived out the urgent response of true faith: recognizing the need to follow the Good Shepherd. Their journey to Bethlehem illustrates that a meaningful life begins with a humble heart willing to seek Jesus. How awesome it is that God's story brings the lowly shepherds to see Jesus and tell others what they had seen. God often uses unlikely people in unlikely ways. These shepherds, often viewed as the lowest in society, needed to embrace their identity as sheep, following the angel's message.

Dear friend, like the shepherds, we are called to go to the manger. In a world that values self-sufficiency and independence, it can be hard to embrace our need for Jesus. But just as the shepherds left their flocks behind, we must set aside our pride and acknowledge our need for guidance. Self-sufficiency will never lead us to the manger. To live fully, we must learn to pause, listen, seek, and follow. The shepherds left their flocks behind, demonstrating that to live fully, we must first acknowledge our own need for guidance. Just as they hurried to the manger, we are called to seek Jesus, recognizing that our strength and wisdom come from Him alone. In doing so, we transform from independent wanderers into eager followers, ready to share the good news of what we've encountered with others. As we identify as sheep, let us remain close to God's voice, asking daily: What do I need to stop doing to follow Jesus more closely?

**Journal:** Reflect on something you need to stop doing in order to follow Jesus more closely. How can letting go of this allow you to better seek His guidance and embrace His purpose for your life?

**One-sentence prayer:** Heavenly Father, help me recognize my need for You as my Good Shepherd.

***Further hope and encouragement: Luke 2:8-20***

# DAY 65
# Don't Let Your Arms Down

*As long as Moses held up his hands, the Israelites were winning;*
*but whenever he lowered his hands, the Amalekites were winning.*
*Exodus 17:11*

In Exodus 17:8–13, we get a powerful picture of what prayer looks like in real life. Moses stood on the hill with his hands raised while a battle was unfolding below. Joshua was on the front lines, leading the charge with a sword as he fought the Amalekites. As long as Moses' hands stayed up, the Israelites were winning. But when he got tired and let them fall, the Amalekites were winning. His raised hands weren't just a symbolic gesture—they were an act of prayer, of interceding, of standing in the gap. It was a physical reminder that what happens in prayer impacts what happens on the ground. And truthfully, that kind of praying is hard. It takes effort. It's not flashy or loud, but it's real work.

We often think the "real work" of life is in the doing—solving problems, showing up, pushing through. But the unseen work of prayer is what holds so much of it together. Moses' story also reminds us that we're not meant to carry this weight alone. When he got tired, Aaron and Hur stood beside him, each holding up an arm. What a picture of community—of people willing to step in when we can't hold it together on our own. The Israelites still had to fight the battle, but prayer played a critical role in their victory. The same is true for us. Life is full of daily battles, and the best way we can show up for others is to pray—consistently, intentionally, and together. And when you feel like you can't keep them up, don't be afraid to let someone else step in and help hold them high. Don't let your arms down.

**Journal:** Who in your life needs your prayers today? How can you be intentional in interceding for them?

**One-Sentence Prayer:** Heavenly Father, help me to never grow weary in standing in the gap for others.

*Further hope and encouragement: Exodus 17:8-16*

## DAY 66
# Follow Me

*Follow Me and I will make you fishers of men.*
*Matthew 4:19*

We live in a culture that celebrates followers, encouraging us to seek validation through social media and personal achievements. It's tempting to focus on ourselves—chasing likes, recognition, or following worldly influence. But the most significant "follow" we could ever pursue is following Jesus, who said, "I am the way, the truth, and the life. No one comes to the Father except through Me" (John 14:6). Following Jesus isn't a one-click thing and you're done. We can't earn anything by what we do on our own, but it still takes effort to follow Jesus, and through God's grace, we can. The word "disciple" literally means "learner," and that's exactly what we are—lifelong learners, growing to become more like Christ. To learn and be shaped by Him, we must stay rooted in the Word of God and follow Him with full obedience. This calling isn't just for a season—it's for a lifetime. When Jesus said, "Follow Me" to the disciples, they did just that—walking, talking, listening, praying, and studying with Him. It was a daily journey of growing in faith and aligning their hearts with His. As one inmate told me about his time before entering San Quentin Rehabilitation Center, "I've always been a believer, but I haven't always been a follower."

Many schools have mission statements emphasizing the importance of cultivating lifelong learners. That principle resonates deeply with me—especially when I think about our walk with Christ. Just as we encourage students to embrace learning beyond the classroom, we are called to keep growing in our faith in Jesus, no matter our age or stage of life. We are finite people following an infinite God, which means there is always more to learn, more to experience, and more of Him to reflect. This is the heart of discipleship—constantly being shaped by Jesus and sharing His love with those around us. To learn and be shaped by Him, we must stay rooted in the Word of God and follow Him with full obedience. As Colossians 1:10 reminds us, "So that you may live a life worthy of the Lord and please Him in every way: bearing fruit in every good work, growing in the knowledge of God." Following Him brings a depth of purpose and joy that no achievement or earthly status could ever offer. Follow Jesus today.

**Journal:** Consider your journey as a lifelong learner and follower of Jesus. How can you commit today to growing in your faith and leading others by example?

**One-sentence prayer:** Heavenly Father, in a world thirsty for followers, I want to follow You.

*Further hope and encouragement: Matthew 4:18-20*

# DAY 67
# Iron Sharpens Iron

*As iron sharpens iron, so one man sharpens another.*
*Proverbs 27:17*

Life can often feel overwhelming, and it's easy to believe that we must face everything on our own. The world will encourage us to be strong, independent, and to handle our struggles quietly. But the truth is, we were never meant to do life alone. Just as iron sharpens iron, we are designed to grow, refine, and strengthen one another through relationships. In Proverbs 27:17, Solomon shares that "as iron sharpens iron, so one person sharpens another." This highlights the importance of having people in our lives who challenge us, encourage us, and help us grow. We all need others who speak truth into our lives, who hold us accountable, and who help us see things from a different perspective. These relationships are crucial for our personal and spiritual growth.

Life doesn't have to be a lonely journey. When we intentionally seek out connections that challenge and encourage us, we create space for growth. Iron sharpens iron through friction, and we, too, are shaped and refined through the connections we form with others. These relationships may not always be easy, but they are necessary for our growth. Think about those in your life who push you to be better, who encourage you when you're down, and who hold you accountable. If you don't have someone who sharpens you, identify someone this week who can walk alongside you, offering wisdom and support. Life is meant to be lived in community, where we grow stronger together.

**Journal:** Who sharpens you in life? How can you strengthen those relationships and seek out others who will challenge and encourage you?

**One-sentence prayer:** Heavenly Father, help me surround myself with people who sharpen, encourage, and challenge me to grow.

***Further hope and encouragement: Proverbs 27***

# DAY 68
# Big Moments

*Commit to the Lord whatever you do, and he will establish your plans.*
*Proverbs 16:3*

I had the privilege of witnessing a former student and basketball player I coached in junior high reach an incredible milestone—scoring her 1,000th collegiate point with a beautiful three-point shot from the right wing. It was a moment of celebration, filled with joy and pride as friends and family cheered from the bleachers holding up a 1,000 point banner. What struck me most as I sat there wasn't just the achievement itself, but the journey it represented. Behind that big moment were countless smaller, mundane ones: the early morning practices, the drills repeated thousands of times, the late-night study sessions balanced with workouts, and even the challenges and hardships that shaped her as a basketball player, and, more importantly, as a person. I can still picture her as a seventh grader in the gym and classroom, working day in and day out as hard as she could in whatever she did, always with a smile on her face. These small, unseen moments of hard work, discipline, and growth laid the foundation for her success. They weren't always glamorous, but they mattered—preparing her for the big moment.

Proverbs 16:3 reminds us, "Commit to the Lord whatever you do, and he will establish your plans." Life is primarily lived in the mundane. It's in the daily tasks of preparation, persistence, and faithfulness that we grow and build character. We often focus on the big moments—those milestones of success or crisis that define our journey. But it's the quiet consistency of showing up, building relationships, and staying true to our calling that prepares us for those defining moments. Like David in the shepherd fields, Joseph in prison, and Moses in the wilderness, the mundane seasons are when God shapes our character, builds trust, and prepares us for the big moments of life. Just as my former player didn't achieve her milestone overnight, we don't thrive in pivotal moments without first stewarding the ordinary ones well. Keep committing your everyday efforts to the Lord, trusting that He uses even the mundane to prepare us for the extraordinary.

**Journal:** Reflect on the small, everyday tasks and moments that contribute to your growth. How can you commit your routine efforts to the Lord, trusting that He is preparing you for the bigger moments ahead?

**One-sentence prayer:** Heavenly Father, I commit all I do to You.

*Further hope and encouragement: Proverbs 16*

# DAY 69
# Solid Rock

*Therefore, everyone who hears these words of mine and puts them into practice is like a wise man who built his house on the rock. The rain came down, the streams rose, and the winds blew and beat against that house; yet it did not fall, because it had its foundation on the rock.*
*Matthew 7:24-25*

One September, my family went to Ocean City, New Jersey, to celebrate my mom's birthday. As we walked toward the beach, the tide was unusually high, reaching almost to the boardwalk. Signs warned us to stay out of the water because of dangerous currents and riptides. While I played it safe and kept my feet on the sand, my brother-in-law dove right in. Not long after, lifeguards called him and the others who had entered the water over to them. I was secretly hoping they were getting kicked out of the water. Instead, the two lifeguards explained, "To your left is a line of rocks. You can't see them now, but they're there." Later that afternoon, as the tide receded, the rocks became visible, stretching out like a solid wall. Before long, we found ourselves standing on them finding seashells and beach glass.

That moment stuck with me, reminding me of God as our Rock. When the waves were crashing, the tide was high, and the currents were pulling, the rocks were hidden—but still present. Isn't that how it feels with God sometimes? When the waves of life crash in and the waters rise, we may not see Him clearly. Yet He is right there. God isn't just above our circumstances—He's right in the midst of them with us. Even when life feels overwhelming with its constant demands and shifting tides, God is steady, offering unshakable strength and peace. Whether you're experiencing high tide or low tide today, know this: the Rock is firm, unchanging, and ever present. Even when you can't see it, He's working for your good and His glory.

**Journal:** When have you faced overwhelming challenges in life? What helped you find stability and strength in those moments? How can you remind yourself that God, your Rock, is always present—even when He feels hidden in the waves?

**One-sentence prayer:** Heavenly Father, You are the Solid Rock on which I stand.

*Further hope and encouragement: Matthew 7:24-29*

# DAY 70
# Water with the Word

*On the last and greatest day of the festival, Jesus stood and said in a loud voice, "Let anyone who is thirsty come to me and drink. Whoever believes in me, as Scripture has said, rivers of living water will flow from within them."*
*John 7:37-38*

We use a dehumidifier in our basement. Part of my daily routine includes a morning workout and emptying the dehumidifier. One summer, Carly asked me to use that water to nourish the two planters on our front porch. Day after day, I watered them, and the plants thrived—growing full and vibrant. But as I began exercising outside more often, my dehumidifier routine slipped. I didn't make the extra effort to go downstairs and empty it, and I watered the plants less and less. I'm sure Carly would tell you that sounds like something I would do! Before long, they began to wither, losing their fullness and beauty. They were thirsty, wilting, and weak—just like we can be when we stop nourishing ourselves. Eventually, I began watering them consistently again, and the plants were restored with new life.

We can't afford to stop "watering" ourselves. It must become a daily habit to pour into our spiritual lives with intention. Just like those planters on the front porch, our growth depends on consistent care. Water yourself with the Word to draw closer to God, finding strength and renewal in Him day by day. When we nurture our relationship with Him, it overflows into our relationships, decisions, and daily interactions. Jesus is the Living Water—He fills, refreshes, and sustains us in ways this world never can. Without Him, we dry up. But with Him, rivers of living water flow through us to bless others. Hydrate your soul today, and let His Word restore your spirit and refresh your life.

**Journal:** How do you make time to consistently "water" your spiritual life? When you find yourself in a dry season, how can you remember the importance of returning to the Living Water of God's Word for renewal and strength?

**One-sentence prayer:** Heavenly Father, water me with Your Word today so I can grow and pour into others.

*Further hope and encouragement: John 4:1-15,*
*Psalm 119:105, Joshua 1:8*

# DAY 71
# Sword of the Spirit

*Take the helmet of salvation and the sword of the Spirit,*
*which is the Word of God.*
*Ephesians 6:17*

Not only did Carly and I use the dehumidifier water to help the plants grow, but its primary purpose was to fight against moisture and mold in the basement. But as young homeowners, we made a mistake—we went nearly twelve years without having a dehumidifier in our underground basement. Everything seemed fine until one day, Carly called me downstairs to show me the walls. When we looked closely, we saw they were covered in tiny black spots—and some not so tiny. The walls had become layered with mold. This wasn't something that happened overnight. It had been building for years, unseen, until it became visibly obvious.

Like the dehumidifier, the Bible is both a tool and a weapon to fight off the "mold" that can grow in our hearts and minds. The sin, doubt, and distractions in our lives don't always show up right away. They often creep in slowly, subtle and unnoticed, until one day they take over. The Word doesn't just help us grow—it helps protect us. It clears out what doesn't belong and keeps our hearts and minds aligned with truth. The Word of God is more than a source of encouragement; it's our defense. Be in the Word, know the Word, and memorize the Word, so the Holy Spirit can bring it to life at the exact moment you need it. Just like the dehumidifier was essential for clearing out our basement, the Word is essential for clearing out your life. Let the sword of the Spirit not just be in your possession, but in your heart—ready to combat the challenges you face each day.

**Journal:** In what areas of your life do you see the subtle "mold" of distractions, sin, or doubt creeping in? What might you be missing or not seeing that is allowing these things to grow? How can you use the sword of the Spirit more effectively to guard against these influences and strengthen your spiritual foundation?

**One-sentence prayer:** Heavenly Father, thank You for giving me Your Word as my sword and strength.

***Further hope and encouragement: Ephesians 6:10-19***

## DAY 72

# When You Fast

*When you fast, do not look somber as the hypocrites do, for they
disfigure their faces to show others they are fasting.
Truly I tell you, they have received their reward in full.*
*Matthew 6:16*

Let me be open about a personal struggle: self-control. Specifically, a lack of self-control when it comes to eating. Carly often teases me about how much I can eat while still managing to "hide it" thanks to my 6'3" frame. I can put on an impressive eating display in the evening but am humbled the next morning when I look in the trashcan or see the empty bowls in the sink. In life, we all face stress and pressure, and in those moments, it's easy to seek comfort in temporary things. For me, it's the cupboards and habitually scrolling through my phone. For you, it might be something else—social media, Netflix, or even overworking. The truth is, these habits can quickly fill spaces that God desires to occupy.

Notice in today's verse that Jesus doesn't say, "if" you fast, but "when" you fast. He assumes it will be part of our spiritual life. Fasting isn't just about abstaining from food; it's about creating intentional space to connect with God. While we often hear about the health benefits of intermittent fasting or fasting for physical well-being, Jesus challenges us to fast with a purpose. Author Donald Whitney (2014) said, "Fasting can be an expression of finding your greatest pleasure and enjoyment in life from God." Think about an area in your life where you're struggling and consider replacing that with fasting. If food isn't the challenge, maybe it's screen time, excessive spending, or even a habit of saying "yes" to too many commitments. Whatever it is, use that time and energy to press into God—the One who can fully satisfy every need and hunger.

**Journal:** What is one area where you tend to seek comfort or control apart from God? How can you incorporate fasting to draw closer to Him this week?

**One-sentence prayer:** Heavenly Father, help me surrender what distracts me from You.

*Further hope and encouragement: Matthew 6*

## DAY 73

# Do All Things Without Complaining

*Do everything without complaining.*
*Philippians 2:14*

Complaining is a culture killer. It seeps into every corner of our lives—our homes, workplaces, churches, conversations at the grocery store, and even casual gatherings at the local coffee shop. It's easy to fall into the trap of venting about our frustrations, whether about long lines, traffic, people, difficult coworkers, or even things we can't control. And yet, complaining has a way of draining the energy and morale of those around us. What starts as a simple vent can quickly turn into a cycle that feeds negativity, both in us and those with whom we interact. As much as I dislike hearing complaints from others, I've come to realize that I can be just as guilty. Whether through my words, my heart, or my thoughts, I often find myself slipping into the very habit I want to avoid.

As Christians, we're called to something higher: to do everything without complaining (Philippians 2:14). Not just some things, not just the easy things, but *everything*. It can feel impossible in a world filled with so many frustrations and challenges, but God invites us to adopt a different mindset. Take today as an opportunity to pay close attention to your thoughts and words. Notice when a complaint starts to form in your mind or when it's about to spill from your lips. Then, pause, and give it to God. Transform those complaints into praise. While we can't control the attitudes or words of others, we can control our own responses. Our hearts overflow with what we choose to fill them with. So, check your thoughts today—are they filled with complaints, or are they overflowing with gratitude? Let's be intentional today and do all things without complaining.

**Journal:** What are some practical steps you can take today to transform complaints into praise in your everyday life? How can you lead by example and create a culture of gratitude wherever you go, whether at home, work, or in your community?

**One-sentence prayer:** Heavenly Father, because of who You are and all You've done, I have nothing to complain about.

**Further hope and encouragement: Philippians 2:12-18, Proverbs 18:21**

# DAY 74
# Welcome Them

*But the crowds learned about it and followed him. He welcomed them and spoke about the kingdom of God and healed those who needed healing.*
*Luke 9:11*

As a principal, one question I often hear is, "Do you have a minute?" That question usually comes at the busiest moments—when I feel like I don't even have a second to spare. I'll come in early to work in the quiet, only to hear the door open, footsteps approaching, and a head popping in: "Hey, I wanted to catch you before the day gets started." Other times, I'm walking out of a difficult conversation or rushing to a crisis when someone asks, "Do you have a minute?" These moments often derail my carefully planned day, leaving me scrambling to keep up. It happens at home, too. Maybe you've been there—you wake up early with a plan, ready for some quiet time, a cup of coffee, and a head start on the day. But just as you settle in, your young child wakes up early, too, needing something from you. Suddenly, the direction you were headed shifts. Sometimes the interruption comes in the form of a phone call or a text message—a friend who's hurting, a family member who needs help, a complete stranger, or someone simply reaching out, needing more than just a quick reply. You had your day mapped out, but one message changes the course.

Prepare to be interrupted today. In Luke 9, Jesus and His disciples withdrew, likely seeking rest after ministering from village to village. But their retreat didn't last long: "The crowds learned about it and followed him" (Luke 9:11). While the disciples wanted to send the crowds away, Jesus responded differently. He welcomed them. Motivated by compassion, Jesus didn't turn them aside or tell them to come back later. So today, plan your day—but hold it loosely. When someone asks for a minute, give them two. When your day is disrupted, respond with grace. Let every interruption become an invitation—to slow down, show love, and welcome others like Jesus did.

**Journal:** How do you typically respond to interruptions in your day? How can you shift your perspective to see these moments as opportunities to show compassion and serve others, just as Jesus did?

**One-sentence prayer:** Heavenly Father, help me see You in the interruptions today.

***Further hope and encouragement: Luke 9:11-17, Matthew 25:34-43***

# DAY 75
# Strength in Connection

*Though one may be overpowered, two can defend themselves.*
*A cord of three strands is not quickly broken.*
*Ecclesiastes 4:12*

I often share about a difficult season in my life when I battled anxiety and depression. I spent countless sleepless nights wrestling with terrible thoughts in my mind. During that time, God drew me closer to Him through His Word and prayer. For months, I walked with God by reading the Bible and talking to Him, but the relief from my struggles didn't come instantly. Then, through God's grace and sovereignty, I had an anxiety attack in public and passed out. What I had been hiding for so long was suddenly out in the open. At first, I felt ashamed and exposed. But over time, I realized that hiding my story had left me feeling isolated, while sharing it made me feel connected.

Notice that I said through God's grace. It wasn't comfortable—but God's grace doesn't always look like comfort. God knew I needed something I was trying to avoid: community. I thought I had to remain "strong" and handle things on my own. But our relational God knew I needed people in my life. Satan thrives in isolation, but God calls us into the light—into connection with others. That anxiety attack, though terrifying at the time, became a turning point. I wouldn't go back and change it if I could. Through His care, God taught me I wasn't meant to walk through life alone. When I shared my story, I discovered I wasn't alone—far from it. God made us for connection—to live in community with one another. Vulnerability isn't a sign of weakness; it's the pathway to strength through Him and through others.

**Journal:** What steps can you take today to embrace vulnerability in your personal and professional relationships? How can you encourage others to lean into connection and build a support system that reflects the strength found in shared experiences?

**One-sentence prayer:** Heavenly Father, help me embrace vulnerability and trust in the strength You provide through community.

*Further hope and encouragement: Ecclesiastes 4:9-12*

# DAY 76
# One Another Living

*Be devoted to one another in love. Honor one another above yourselves.*
*Romans 12:10*

Today's devotion is simple but vital. We are made for community. And yet, if you're anything like me, there are times when you'd rather be alone or only surrounded by those who make you feel comfortable. Relationships can be messy, and it's easy to avoid the discomfort they sometimes bring. But God's Word is clear: we are called to live in community, to seek the best interests of others above our own. Today, let's reflect on the powerful message of "one another" and what God calls us to do in our everyday lives:

+ Love one another (John 13:34-35)
+ Serve one another (Galatians 5:13)
+ Bear one another's burdens (1 Thessalonians 5:11)
+ Forgive one another (Ephesians 4:32)
+ Be kind to one another (Ephesians 4:32)
+ Consider one another (Hebrews 10:24)
+ Confess your sins to one another (James 5:16)
+ Show hospitality to one another (1 Peter 4:9)
+ Clothe yourself with humility to one another (1 Peter 5:5)
+ Live in harmony with one another (Romans 12:16)
+ Be devoted to one another (Romans 12:10)

Whether at home, at work, in your neighborhood, or anywhere life takes you, these "one another" commands remind us that life is not meant to be lived in isolation. We are called to relationships—to love deeply, serve selflessly, and live with humility. When we invest in others, we reflect the heart of Christ and help create spaces where trust, unity, and joy can grow. Today, let's commit to living in ways that elevate others, honoring them above ourselves, and radiating the love of Christ in every interaction.

**Journal:** How can you actively live out the "one another" principles today? What steps can you take to foster a life marked by love, compassion, and kindness?

**One-sentence prayer:** Heavenly Father, help me to love, serve, and honor others today.

***Further hope and encouragement: Romans 12***

# DAY 77
# It's Yours, Lord

*The earth is the Lord's, and everything in it, the world, and all who live in it.*
*Psalm 24:1*

Every morning, I'm blessed with the opportunity to take my oldest daughter to the bus stop. As she steps out of the truck and walks toward the bus, she always looks back with a quick wave and a smile. It's a small, sweet moment—but it holds so much meaning. I make sure I'm never looking down, because I don't want to miss it. As I watch her climb the steps, I'm reminded of when she first boarded the bus as a kindergartener, her backpack nearly as big as she was. Now a middle schooler, she walks with confidence, and the bus steps don't seem quite as giant—but I still whisper the same prayer every single day: "She's Yours, Lord." It's a humbling reminder that, no matter her age or stage, I am not in control—God is. He holds her life, her steps, and her future in His hands. That moment each morning shapes how I live, and it also drives me in my role as a school principal. Families send schools their best every day, and I want to honor that trust by caring for each student to the best of my ability. I often pray, "They're Yours, Lord," over the students and staff in the building, trusting that He loves and leads them far better than I ever could.

This daily routine at the bus stop has become a powerful reminder of trust and surrender. Psalm 24:1 grounds this truth: "The earth is the Lord's, and everything in it, the world, and all who live in it." The people in our lives—our children, friends, coworkers, students, family members—are not ours to control or carry alone. They belong to God. Our role is to steward well what He has entrusted to us, approaching each day with an "It's Yours, Lord" mindset. Surrender isn't about giving up—it's about giving over. Just as I release my daughter into God's care each morning as she boards the bus, we are invited to entrust every part of our lives—our families, our work, our challenges—to the One who loves perfectly and leads faithfully. It's yours, Lord. It's all Yours.

**Journal:** How can you approach today with an "It's Yours, Lord" mindset? What areas of your life are you holding too tightly? How can you surrender control and trust God with what—and who—matters most?

**One-sentence prayer:** Heavenly Father, It's Yours Lord, You are in control.

***Further hope and encouragement: Psalm 24***

## DAY 78
# Stay Disciplined

*Now when Daniel learned that the decree had been published, he went home to his upstairs room where the windows opened toward Jerusalem. Three times a day he got down on his knees and prayed, giving thanks to his God, just as he had done before.*
*Daniel 6:10*

Life is full of choices that test our resolve, and as Jim Rohn (n.d.) is often quoted, "We must all suffer from one of two pains: the pain of discipline or the pain of regret." This truth has proven itself time and again in my own life. Discipline, while often difficult in the moment, is far lighter to bear than the heavy weight of regret. Whether it's choosing to prioritize health by skipping a late-night snack, staying focused through an overwhelming to-do list instead of procrastinating, or making a tough call or having a difficult conversation rather than avoiding it—discipline demands effort, but it spares us the lingering sting of "what-ifs" or "why did I do that?" That doesn't mean it's easy. I've certainly been tempted to cut corners, delay decisions, or settle for convenience. But time has taught me that regret—especially when it comes from inaction or compromise—always weighs more heavily on the heart. Choosing discipline in daily life doesn't just build consistency; it strengthens our character and deepens our trust in God.

Scripture offers powerful examples of this principle in action. In 2 Samuel 11, King David's failure to stay disciplined led to consequences following his sin with Bathsheba. One lapse in judgment led to deep regret and consequences that affected his entire kingdom. On the other hand, Daniel shows us the fruit of steady faithfulness. Despite the threat of being thrown into the lion's den, he remained committed to prayer and his relationship with God. His discipline didn't just keep him grounded—it shaped his legacy and impacted others. Whether you're parenting, working, leading, or simply trying to grow in your walk with Christ, discipline plays a vital role. A life rooted daily in God's Word and steady in prayer aligns our hearts with His will. Choose the lighter burden today by staying disciplined—spiritual disciplines take effort, but they're worth it. They'll shape your life—and your witness—for your greatest good and God's glory.

**Journal:** Where in your life are you being called to stay disciplined today? What choices may feel difficult now but will help you avoid the weight of regret later? How can your daily routines, like Daniel's commitment to prayer, help anchor you in faith and purpose?

**One-sentence prayer:** Heavenly Father, help me stay disciplined and honor You today.

*Further hope and encouragement: 1 Corinthians 9:24-27, Daniel 6*

# DAY 79
# Eyes that See

*Calling his disciples to him, Jesus said, "Truly I tell you, this poor widow has put more into the treasury than all the others. They all gave out of their wealth; but she, out of her poverty, put in everything—all she had to live on."*
*Mark 12:43-44*

Life is full of moments that are easy to miss or overlook—especially in the small, seemingly insignificant acts of service. I think of Kim, the cafeteria worker at school. Day after day, she quietly serves meals, greeting every student with a kind word. Between serving food, she scrubs counters, mops floors, and keeps the kitchen spotless. Her dedication can easily go unnoticed amidst the busyness of the day, but when you take a moment to observe, you realize her work is extraordinary. Life is about seeing people like Kim—those whose consistent efforts reflect integrity and commitment—and letting them know their work matters. A kind word, a simple note, or even just acknowledging their efforts can make all the difference.

In Scripture, Jesus exemplifies this by seeing the unnoticed. He recognized the widow who put two small coins into the temple treasury (Mark 12:41-44). While others dismissed her offering as insignificant, Jesus praised her faithfulness, acknowledging her sacrifice. In life, we're called to follow His example. Philippians 2:4 reminds us, "Let each of you look not only to his own interests, but also to the interests of others." By focusing on others—whether in the workplace, at home, or in our communities—we can transform the culture around us. A quick thank-you, a word of encouragement, or a small act of service can serve as a reflection of Christ's love and grace. Life isn't about being seen—it's about seeing others the way Jesus sees them. Take time today to notice and appreciate the "little" things; they often reveal God's heart and make the biggest difference.

**Journal:** Think about someone in your life whose contributions often go unnoticed. How can you show appreciation for their efforts today? Reflect on how recognizing the "small" things can impact those around you and the overall culture of your home, workplace, or community.

**One-sentence prayer:** Heavenly Father, help me see others as You see them, valuing their quiet contributions and showing Your love through my actions today.

***Further hope and encouragement: Mark 12:41-44***

# DAY 80
# Use Them

*Then I heard the voice of the Lord saying, 'Whom shall I send?*
*And who will go for us?' And I said, 'Here am I. Send me.*
Isaiah 6:8

I met Alisabeth during a trip to the Dominican Republic at her small sewing shop. From a worldly perspective, she doesn't have much, but if you take the time to talk with her, you'll quickly realize—she has everything. Her sewing business began when she felt a stirring in her heart, a realization that she had more to offer the world. That's when she decided to step out in faith and start her own business. Her words should resonate deeply with all of us: "God has given me gifts and talents. I must use them." She felt the Lord's call on her life, and she answered. Her dream for her children is simple yet profound: that they work hard, using the gifts God has given them, to serve Him.

Alisabeth's story is a powerful reminder of Isaiah 6:8, when the Lord asked, "Whom shall I send?" and Isaiah responded, "Here am I. Send me." Like Isaiah, Alisabeth didn't hesitate—she heard God's call and stepped forward in faith. She didn't wait for the perfect moment, ideal circumstances, or more resources. Instead, she said, "Here I am, Lord. Use me." And because of her obedience, God is working through her life. God has given each of us unique talents and abilities—not for our own gain, but for His glory and the advancement of His kingdom. The question is: are we using them? Don't waste what He has entrusted to you. Don't look back with regret, saying, "I wish I would have," "I should have," or "I could have." Like Alisabeth in her small sewing room on the streets of Santo Domingo, faithfully stewarding her gifts, we, too, must step forward in obedience. Stop waiting for the perfect time—there is no perfect time. Actually, there is—right now. Where is God calling you? Have you taken the time to pause and truly listen? Be like Alisabeth. Answer the call, step into what He has already placed in your hands, and watch Him work. He has given you gifts and talents—now, through God's grace, it's up to you to use them.

**Journal:** What talents and gifts has God given you? Are you fully using them for His glory, or are there areas where you've been hesitant to step out in faith? Write about one step you can take this week to use your gifts in obedience to His calling.

**One-sentence prayer:** Heavenly Father, help me to hear Your call clearly and respond with boldness, using the gifts You have given me for Your purpose.

***Further hope and encouragement: Isaiah 6:1-8***

## DAY 81
# Love Your Family Well

*Anyone who does not provide for their relatives, and especially for their*
*own household, has denied the faith and is worse than an unbeliever.*
1 Timothy 5:8

It was Friday night, and I was ready to rest after a long week. But as my head hit the pillow, guilt replaced my anticipation of sleep. Just hours earlier, I had tweeted, "Go home and love your family." It felt good to encourage others to prioritize their loved ones. But as I laid there, I realized I hadn't lived out my own words. I had gone home and scrolled my phone while my family sat in the living room. I had been impatient and distracted. The very people God had entrusted to me—the ones who mattered most—had received less of me than my work had that week.

It's easy to pour ourselves into our roles and responsibilities, justifying long hours and distraction by telling ourselves it's for our family's benefit or it's part of our purpose. But Scripture calls us to be stewards of what God places right in front of us—and far too often, those are the people we miss. Paul's letter to Timothy reminds us that neglecting our families undermines our faith. Loving them well isn't an add-on to a meaningful life—it's central to it. Jesus modeled this so clearly. Even in the middle of His ministry, He paused to care for those nearest to Him. If we lose our family's trust and connection while chasing success outside the home, we're not leading—we're losing. And the same applies within our church family. When we overlook those in our community who are lonely, hurting, or in need, we miss an opportunity to reflect the heart of Christ. Life isn't only about what happens at work or in public. It's about what happens in the living room, around the dinner table, and in the small moments where we choose presence over productivity. Let's lead—and live—where it matters most: by loving our families well.

**Journal:** Reflect on a recent moment when you were distracted or impatient with your family. How can you prioritize quality time with them in the midst of your busy schedule? Consider how loving your family well can strengthen your relationships and impact both at home and beyond.

**One-sentence prayer:** Heavenly Father, help me reflect Jesus in the way I love my family.

***Further hope and encouragement: 1 Timothy 5***

# DAY 82
# Solitude and Community

*After leaving them, he went up on a mountainside and prayed.*
*Mark 6:46*

You may be thinking, "This devotional encourages me to make time for solitude, but it also emphasizes the importance of staying connected with others and being in community. So, should I be with people or by myself? I'm confused." You're not confused—you're absolutely right. Life often feels like a delicate balance between time alone and time spent with others. God's Word is good, and it is a lamp to our feet and a light for our path (Psalm 119:105). Jesus perfectly modeled the balance of solitude and community, showing us that both are essential for a full and meaningful life.

In life, we must learn to follow Jesus' example: stepping away for moments of quiet reflection with God and then re-entering community to connect with and serve others. Sometimes I feel like I'm both an introvert and an extrovert—I'm energized by time with people, but I also crave moments of stillness. Life requires both. If we don't take time to withdraw, we risk running on empty, disconnected from the One who fills us. But if we withdraw for too long, we miss the chance to pour into others and fulfill our purpose. We must find a rhythm that includes both—a rhythm of withdrawing to be alone with God and a rhythm of engaging in community. Some may need brief moments of solitude each day, while others might need longer retreats when necessary. Ask yourself today: What is your rhythm? Are you intentionally making space to recharge in solitude? Are you stepping into community to connect, collaborate, and support others? Jesus invites you to embrace both. When you follow His example, you'll find balance, renewal, and strength for all areas of life.

**Journal:** Reflect on your rhythm of solitude and community. Are you making time to recharge alone *and* connect with others? How can you adjust your schedule to prioritize both?

**One-sentence prayer:** Heavenly Father, show me when to withdraw and when to re-enter.

*Further hope and encouragement: Luke 5:16,*
*Matthew 14:23, Matthew 22:37-39*

## DAY 83
# Talking to Ourselves

*Finally, brothers and sisters, whatever is true, whatever is noble,*
*whatever is right, whatever is pure, whatever is lovely, whatever is admirable—*
*if anything is excellent or praiseworthy—think about such things.*
*Philippians 4:8*

Carly is always talking to herself. But here's the thing: the times I think she's talking to herself, I won't say anything, and she'll say, "Zac, I'm talking to you!" The times I think she's telling me something, I'll ask her what she said, and she responds with, "I'm talking to myself." I can't seem to ever get it right. She has a soft tone to her voice, so sometimes I miss what she's saying, even if she's right in front of me. Add in the fact that I don't hear well out of my left ear (she calls it selective hearing), and it leads to plenty of confusion around our house. When I'm not sure what she's saying, I just try to smile and nod in agreement...it only works some of the time.

All joking aside, no one talks to us more than we do. What are we telling ourselves? The thoughts in our minds and the words on our tongues overflow from what's stored in our hearts. Are we speaking truth to ourselves—filling our minds with hope, love, encouragement, and grace? Or are we letting fear, doubt, and anxiety take over the conversation? Colossians 3:2 urges us to set our minds on "things above." Our self-talk matters. It shapes how we see the world and how we walk through it. When our inner dialogue is grounded in truth, we can move through life with clarity, confidence, and peace. But if we're not careful, we'll start to echo the noise around us. So, what are we feeding our minds? Is it social media, breaking news, and constant noise—or are we making space for the life-giving Word of God to renew us from the inside out? It sounds simple, but it's true: what we fill our minds with is what will be on our minds. Let's choose to speak life today. Because what we say to ourselves matters.

**Journal:** What are the recurring thoughts you tell yourself—both positive and negative? How can you intentionally replace any lies, fears, or doubts with truth to live with greater confidence and peace?

**One-sentence prayer:** Heavenly Father, help me align my thoughts with Your truth today.

*Further hope and encouragement: Philippians 4:1-9, Colossians 3:1-2*

## DAY 84
# Calm Yourself on the Way

*And the peace of God, which transcends all understanding,*
*will guard your hearts and your minds in Christ Jesus.*
*Philippians 4:7*

Early in my career, I had the privilege of working under someone who modeled grace under pressure. Whenever a crisis arose—a student in distress, an upset parent, or a colleague needing immediate support—he would gently remind me, "Calm yourself on the way." He taught me to pause, take a deep breath, collect my thoughts, and offer a quick prayer before stepping into the situation. By the time I arrived, I was better able to bring calm to the chaos, helping others feel seen and supported in the middle of their stress. His wisdom taught me that our composure often sets the tone for how others respond.

In life, we're often called to be a calming presence, but that peace doesn't come from ourselves—it comes from Christ. Jesus is our ultimate calm in the chaos. When the disciples were terrified in the storm, Jesus spoke, "Peace, be still," and the winds and waves obeyed (Mark 4:39). When we face challenging situations—a disobedient child, a disagreement with our spouse, a tense moment at work, an upset customer or client, or frustrations while coaching—His peace transcends our understanding (Philippians 4:7). Only through His grace can we pause before reacting, take a breath, and invite His peace to guide us. The simple reminder to "calm yourself on the way" can be a powerful tool when we face moments of frustration. When we respond with His calm, we point others to the One who still calms every storm.

**Journal:** Think of a recent chaotic situation. How did you respond, and how might pausing, praying, and preparing have changed the outcome? Reflect on a time when Jesus brought peace to your storm and how you can rely on Him for future calm.

**One-sentence prayer:** Heavenly Father, help me bring Your peace into every situation I encounter today.

*Further hope and encouragement: Mark 4:35-41*

## DAY 85
# The Mess

*But God demonstrates his own love for us in this:*
*While we were still sinners, Christ died for us.*
*Romans 5:8*

One morning, it hit me. Honestly, it should hit me every morning. The whirlwind of life was in full swing—three kids getting ready for school (Carly would probably say four), crumbs on the counter, breakfast dishes still on the table, clothes scattered across the floor, toothpaste splattered in the sink. Each of us in different moods, different headspaces, trying to get out the door on time. In the middle of it all, Carly moved calmly through the chaos—packing lunches, finding missing shoes, wiping counters, offering encouragement. As we rushed out the door, I couldn't help but reflect on her steady care. No matter the mess we leave behind—physically or emotionally—she meets us with love, grace, and service. It's a quiet, powerful reflection of Jesus.

Life is messy. We live in a broken world, surrounded by imperfect people—ourselves included. And yet, Christ steps right into the middle of it—not with frustration, but with mercy and compassion. He doesn't wait for us to clean things up first. Romans 5:8 reminds us, "While we were still sinners, Christ died for us." Whether it's raising kids, navigating relationships, facing challenges at work, or just making it through the day, we're called to show up with grace, especially when things are messy. The people in our lives—our kids, our coworkers, our neighbors, our friends—they won't always get it right. Neither will we. But just as Jesus meets us in our mess, we're invited to meet others in theirs—with patience, humility, and an open heart. One of my favorite Bob Goff (2018) quotes says, "Love difficult people. You're one of them." Carly lives out the "love difficult people" part daily—hey, she married me. She doesn't wait for the house—or the people in it—to be perfect. She loves and serves anyway. Today, may we do the same. May we live like Jesus—extending grace to even the messiest moments.

**Journal:** Think about a "messy" situation you've faced recently. How did you respond? How might you reflect Christ's grace and compassion more intentionally next time?

**One-sentence prayer:** Heavenly Father, thank You for meeting me in my mess with grace and mercy.

*Further hope and encouragement: Romans 5*

# DAY 86
# The Battle Belongs to God

*This is what the Lord says to you: Do not be afraid or discouraged because of this vast army. For the battle is not yours, but God's.*
1 Chronicles 2:20

Life is full of "battles," both big and small. Think of a battle you're facing right now. Is there something in your life that has you feeling afraid, discouraged, or defeated? What challenges are you up against that seem too overwhelming to face on your own? Maybe you feel like you're stuck in a season where nothing seems to be working, and you're wondering how much longer you can keep going. It could be a tough conversation, a health struggle, a financial hardship, or a broken relationship that weighs heavily on your heart.

Take a deep breath. As you inhale, focus on the battle you're facing. As you exhale, let go of that burden and remind yourself, "The battle belongs to God." Do this for every battle you are facing today. As new challenges arise, pause and exhale the battle to God, trusting that He is already at work, even in the most difficult moments. This doesn't mean that you won't have to make decisions or take action, but it does mean you don't have to face these struggles alone. God is in control, and the outcome is already in His hands. Today, as you face life's battles, remember that God is your ultimate defender, and He's already working on your behalf. So, go out and breathe easier today, knowing that as you face your battles, they belong to Him.

**Journal:** What battles are you facing in your life right now? Whether it's a tough decision, a difficult conversation, or an ongoing struggle, remember that the battle belongs to God. Write down your thoughts and prayers as you turn each of these battles over to Him today.

**One-sentence prayer:** Heavenly Father, the battle belongs to You.

***Further hope and encouragement: 2 Chronicles 20:15-17, Psalm 27***

## DAY 87
# Tell Your Story

*"Go to your family and tell them how much the Lord has
done for you and how he has had mercy on you."*
*Mark 5:19*

In life, it's often said, but rarely done: people admire our strengths but connect with our weaknesses. As I journeyed through a season of anxiety and depression, I had no idea what God was doing in my life. Now, as time has passed and I reflect on that time, it's become clearer that He had a plan for me all along. God used that season to soften and shape my heart, drawing me closer to Him. It was also during that time that He prepared me to walk alongside others facing similar struggles. He gave me empathy and compassion for others that I would not have had without that trial. Just as 2 Corinthians 1:3-4 reminds us, God comforts us in our struggles so that we can comfort others with the same comfort we received. It meant stepping outside of my comfort zone and sharing my story.

What's your story? We each have a unique story—one that God has written to draw us closer to Him and to others. Are we hiding our stories by keeping them to ourselves? Once I began sharing my own, I was amazed at how many others were struggling with similar challenges. Just like Jesus told the man who had been healed, "Go home and tell your family how much the Lord has done for you and how He has had mercy on you" (Mark 5:19), our stories have the power to connect and inspire. When the man shared his story, the people were amazed (Mark 5:20). By following the Good Shepherd and sharing our story, we never know who might be encouraged or inspired by hearing about God's mercy in our lives. Our story has the power to reveal His goodness to others.

**Journal:** What is a significant moment in your life when you've clearly seen God's mercy and goodness? How has that experience shaped who you are? Reflect on who might need to hear your story today and how sharing it could encourage or inspire them.

**One-sentence prayer:** Heavenly Father, You've given me a story—strengthen me to share it.

***Further hope and encouragement: Mark 5:18-20, 2 Corinthians 1:3-4***

## DAY 88
# Grace Over Perfection

*"My grace is sufficient for you, for my power is made perfect in weakness."*
*2 Corinthians 12:9*

As a kid, I loved getting 100% on my assignments. Perfection was the goal, and anything less felt like failure. But as I got a little older, there were times I'd miss one or two questions on an assignment. You'd think I'd still be happy and move on, but I couldn't. Instead, I'd sneak into the garage and throw the paper away before going inside so my parents wouldn't see. It's not like I was failing these assignments, but because it wasn't perfect, I didn't want it to be seen. Years later, I sat with a principal who shared a lesson that stayed with me. He said, "The moment I quit trying to be the perfect principal and started focusing on showing Christ's love to others was when it all clicked for me." That simple, yet profound, truth challenged me to examine my own life. Was I striving for perfection, or was I allowing God's love and grace to guide my actions?

Paul reminds us in 2 Corinthians 12:9, "My grace is sufficient for you, for my power is made perfect in weakness." God doesn't require perfection from us; He extends His grace. In life, we're called to live with grace, not perfection. Our imperfections remind us of our dependence on Him and allow His power to work through us. Looking back, I'm thankful that my worth wasn't defined by a perfect score on assignments or by doing everything right. God doesn't expect perfection, but He equips us to move forward through His grace. Let's embrace grace and growth over perfection, showing Christ's love to others, and trusting that His grace is always sufficient for whatever work He calls us to do.

**Journal:** In what areas of life are you striving for perfection instead of relying on God's grace? How can we shift our focus to showing Christ's love through our actions?

**One-sentence prayer:** Heavenly Father, help me live with grace and show Your love today.

*Further hope and encouragement: 2 Corinthians 12:9*

## DAY 89
# Righteous and Kind

*Because Joseph her husband was faithful to the law, and yet did not want
to expose her to public disgrace, he had in mind to divorce her quietly.*
Matthew 1:19

We see the true character of people when situations become difficult. Growing up, I played on sports teams where moments of adversity revealed who people really were. Some players became frustrated, ready to give up, and let their emotions lead to words and actions they later regretted. Others, however, used those challenges as opportunities to learn, grow, and remain positive, yet realistic. Their attitudes inspired and uplifted the team even in tough times. It taught me an important lesson: who we are when things are not going well defines us more than who we are when things are going well.

Joseph, the earthly father of Jesus, faced one of the greatest challenges a man could experience. He discovered that Mary, pledged to be married to him, was with child—and not by him. Can you imagine the confusion, hurt, and betrayal he might have felt? Yet Scripture describes Joseph as both righteous and kind. He didn't lash out or act on impulse. Instead, he sought to do what was right without exposing Mary to disgrace (we see later in the chapter that an angel visited Joseph and revealed that the baby conceived in Mary was from the Holy Spirit). In one of the most difficult moments of his life, Joseph chose righteousness and kindness. In life, we are called to respond like Joseph, no matter how difficult the situation may be. When things are hard, when tensions run high, and when emotions flare, let's commit to responding with righteousness and kindness. By choosing to be righteous and kind, we reflect God's character and inspire others to do the same, even in adversity.

**Journal:** Think about a recent situation where things got hard. How did you respond? How would others describe the way you responded? Write about how you can choose to respond with righteousness and kindness in future challenges.

**One-sentence prayer:** Heavenly Father, help me to be righteous and kind, no matter the challenges I face.

***Further hope and encouragement: Matthew 1:18-25***

## DAY 90

# Light in the Darkness

*When Jesus spoke again to the people, he said, "I am the light of the world. Whoever follows me will never walk in darkness, but will have the light of life."*
*John 8:12*

I don't know what time of year you're reading this, but I love how Christmas falls near the darkest time of the year. December 21st and 22nd mark the winter solstice—the days with the least amount of sunlight—and December 25th is not far behind. How fitting that we celebrate the birth of Jesus, the Light of the World, in the midst of the darkest days! Many people struggle with the winter blues or seasonal depression (me included), often tied to the lack of light. The contrast between the darkness of the season and the celebration of Christ's light reminds us that His arrival brings hope and joy to a world in deep need.

In John 8:12, Jesus says, "I am the light of the world. Whoever follows me will never walk in darkness but will have the light of life." As followers of Christ, we're called to reflect that light in the way we live, love, and treat others. Many people around us—friends, family, neighbors, coworkers—are facing their own dark days, filled with sadness, anxiety, heartache, or uncertainty. We're not immune to those struggles either. Yet through Jesus, we are equipped to be a beacon of hope, offering encouragement, support, and kindness. Whether it's during the winter season or in the everyday moments of life, let's remember the source of our light. When we feel overwhelmed by our own challenges, may we draw strength from Him. And when we encounter others in need, may our lives shine brightly—pointing them to the Light of the World…Jesus.

**Journal:** Who around you may be walking through a season of darkness? Write about one specific way you can bring light—through encouragement, support, or simple kindness—into their life this week.

**One-sentence prayer:** Heavenly Father, help me reflect Your light wherever I go.

*Further hope and encouragement: John 8:12-20*

# DAY 91
# Just Like Your Father

*Whoever claims to live him must walk as Jesus did*
*1 John 2:6*

There's a lady I know who used to always say to me, "You're just like your father." Rose joked, "You're so much like your father I could slap you" (all in good fun). Of course, she was talking about my earthly father. Her words remind me of a truth: we often become like the people we follow. Think about the coaches, teachers, and leaders who have shaped your life. Do you notice their tendencies in yourself? I recently met with a first-year teacher after observing her excellent lesson. When I praised her, she humbly redirected the credit to her cooperating teacher from student teaching, explaining that much of what she does comes from them. Similarly, when I coach basketball, baseball, or softball, I find myself repeating phrases and running drills just as my coaches did.

Today's verse from 1 John reminds us that whoever claims to live in Christ must walk as Jesus did. As people striving to live faithfully, there's no greater example to follow than Jesus. His life models humility, compassion, and a servant's heart. But to walk as Jesus did, we must first know how Jesus walked. Throughout His time on earth, Jesus constantly aligned Himself vertically with the Father—stepping away to pray, seeking His will, and drawing strength from their relationship. In the same way, we're called to stay connected to God through His Word and in prayer, allowing Him to shape our hearts. We naturally reflect those we follow—and when we follow Jesus, He transforms us from the inside out. Through His grace, we grow to love like Him, serve like Him, and live with His wisdom and kindness. In a world full of uncertainty and need, let's commit to walking as Jesus did—daily aligning ourselves with the Father—so that our lives may reflect His light and love wherever we go. And maybe, just maybe, someone like Rose will smile and say, "You're just like your Father."

**Journal:** Think about the people who have influenced the way you live—teachers, coaches, mentors, or family members. What qualities or habits have you picked up from them? How can you intentionally follow Jesus more closely so that His character is seen in your everyday life?

**One-sentence prayer:** Heavenly Father, help me walk with You today and reflect Your heart in all I do.

*Further hope and encouragement: 1 John 2*

# DAY 92
# Building Castles That Last

*Do not store up for yourselves treasures on earth, where moths
and vermin destroy, and where thieves break in and steal. But store
up for yourselves treasures in heaven, where moths and vermin do
not destroy, and where thieves do not break in and steal.*
Matthew 6:19-20

My family grew up going to the Jersey Shore. I went as a kid, and now we take our kids. When they were younger, one of their favorite things to do was build sandcastles near the shoreline at low tide. All day long, I'd haul buckets of ocean water back and forth—one in each hand—helping bring their sandy vision to life. It was a lot of work! By the end of the day, we had something pretty impressive. But as the tide rolled in, wave after wave crashed into the castle until it was completely washed away. Despite all our effort, there was no sign it had ever existed.

Life can feel a lot like that. We can spend so much time and energy building our own "sandcastles"—chasing success, possessions, popularity, or status. But like that castle on the beach, those things won't last. Eventually, the tide comes in. So what are we really doing with the time we've been given? Are we investing in what matters most, or are we caught up in what's temporary and fleeting? The only work that endures is what we do for God's kingdom—loving others, sharing His truth, living out His grace. When we align our hearts with eternity, we stop striving for recognition and start focusing on relationships. Let's spend our lives building castles that won't wash away—treasures that stand forever in heaven.

**Journal:** What "sandcastles" might be taking your focus? What would it look like to live each day with eternity in mind?

**One-sentence prayer:** Heavenly Father, help me focus on what matters most and build a life that reflects Your eternal love.

*Further hope and encouragement: Matthew 7:24-27*

## DAY 93

# Three Questions

*The Lord will fight for you; you need only to be still*
*Exodus 14:14*

In the hustle and bustle of life, the command to "be still" can feel like a luxury we can't afford. Our natural response tends to be, "Be still? I don't have time for that!" Yet it's a command God has given—for our good and for His glory. My pastor and friend, Michael Brown, often encourages the congregation to ask three powerful questions as we spend time with God in His Word: *Who is God? Who are we in light of who God is? And what has God called us to do?* These questions guide us into a posture of humility, clarity, and purpose. Reflecting on who God is anchors us in His sovereignty, holiness, and love. From that place of awe, we can rightly see ourselves as beloved, yet dependent, children of God—called to align our lives with His will.

Ligon Duncan (n.d) captured it beautifully: "Isn't it interesting that before God calls us to obey, before He calls us to great tasks, He reminds us of who we are in Him?" This truth matters deeply in everyday life. When we neglect to pause, reflect, and meditate on God's Word, we risk moving through life at a hurried pace, relying on our own strength, and losing sight of the One who leads us. Creating space in our day to be still is more than just an act of obedience—it's a lifeline for faithful living. Take time today to pause, be still, and reflect on those three questions. Let them shape how you live, love, serve, and respond to the calling God has placed on your life.

**Journal:** Where in your day can you pause to be still before God? What truths about Him—and about yourself—come into focus when you do?

**One-sentence prayer:** Heavenly Father, help me to pause and be still in Your presence, reflecting on who You are, who I am in You, and what You've called me to do.

***Further hope and encouragement: Exodus 14***

# DAY 94
# Burn Bright, Not Out

*You are the light of the world. A city on a hill cannot be hidden.*
*Matthew 5:14*

My mom throws incredible birthday parties—not just when my sisters and I were kids, but even now for our families and her grandchildren. She even gives us themes. For my 21st birthday, we had a rubber ducky race! Come on, I mean, how many people have rubber ducky races for their 21st birthday? How cool is that? Now, in my late 30s, she still gives me awesome baseball-themed birthdays. The birthday boy or girl always gets to pick the meal and dessert as well. It's a special night. One of the most memorable moments is when it's time for dessert. We gather around for a family picture, and as we begin singing, she starts lighting the candles. She usually lights one candle first and then uses it to light the others. With the dim lighting above the kitchen, that single flame begins to spread, and soon all the candles are glowing, filling the space with light. But every now and then, the first candle goes out before she can light the others, and the room remains dark.

The same is true for us. In Matthew 5:14, Jesus reminds us, "You are the light of the world." We are called to reflect His light in our lives, spreading that light to those around us. Like those birthday candles, we're meant to shine and brighten the world. But if we allow ourselves to burn out—neglecting our emotional, spiritual, and physical well-being—our light dims, and we have nothing left to give. We need to take care of ourselves. It's important to make time for rest, reflection, and renewal so that we can continue shining brightly and fulfilling our purpose. When we stay connected to Christ, we can light up the world around us, just as He intended.

**Journal:** What steps can you take this week to prioritize rest and renewal so your light doesn't burn out? How can you intentionally reflect Christ's light in your daily life?

**One-sentence prayer:** Heavenly Father, keep my light shining bright for You today.

*Further hope and encouragement: Matthew 5:13-16*

## DAY 95

# Building Leaders Who Build Leaders

*"Therefore, go and make disciples of all nations, baptizing them in the name of the Father and of the Son and of the Holy Spirit, and teaching them to obey everything I have commanded you. And surely I am with you always, to the very end of the age."*
*Matthew 28:19-20*

Life is not about what benefits us, but about pursuing the best interests of others. True influence is selfless and rooted in the desire to empower others. However, serving others doesn't always mean doing everything for them. It can be harmful if we try to do everything ourselves. Sometimes, the greatest service we can offer is helping people build their own capacity to lead, solve problems, and grow. Life is not about creating followers; it's about creating leaders. The goal is not to simply solve today's challenges but to equip others with the tools to navigate challenges long after we're gone. This reflects the timeless truth: "Give a man a fish, and he will eat for a day; teach a man to fish, and he will eat for a lifetime." However, great influence takes it a step further: teach a person to teach others to fish, and you create a ripple effect of growth and influence.

Jesus modeled this perfectly with His disciples. He didn't just meet their needs; He taught, mentored, and led them so that they could go out and lead others. Jesus was intentional about equipping His disciples to carry forward His mission. In Matthew 28:19-20, He commissions them to "go and make disciples of all nations," ensuring that His message would continue to spread. We are called to do the same—investing in others, building them up, and preparing them to lead others. Are we equipping those we influence to grow, thrive, and make an impact beyond our direct reach? Today, consider how we are building leaders within leaders.

**Journal:** Who in your circle, or beyond, can you mentor and empower today to lead others in their journey?

**One-sentence prayer:** Heavenly Father, help me lead with intentionality, building leaders who reflect Your love and purpose.

***Further hope and encouragement: Matthew 28***

## DAY 96
# It's God Who Gets the Glory

*"My food," said Jesus, "is to do the will of him*
*who sent me and to finish his work."*
*John 4:34*

One of my favorite quotes is attributed to Harry S. Truman (n.d): "It is amazing what you can accomplish when you do not care who gets the credit." This wisdom resonates deeply in life and teamwork. Think about sports: running backs or quarterbacks often receive public praise for great runs, passes, and touchdowns, yet their success is only made possible by the linemen blocking for them. In basketball, the top scorer grabs the headlines, but the point guard's passes set up those shots. The best teams don't focus on individual glory—they focus on collective success. The same principle applies to all areas of life. The most effective people are those who prioritize the success of the group, celebrating wins for the team rather than seeking recognition for themselves.

Jesus lived this principle perfectly, but He took it one step further: everything He did was to glorify God, not Himself. Throughout His ministry, Jesus constantly redirected attention to His Father in heaven, saying, "My food is to do the will of Him who sent me and to finish His work" (John 4:34). His focus was never on accumulating credit or recognition but on pointing others to God. In life, we are called to the same mission: to work humbly, striving for the success of others, while ultimately seeking to bring glory to God in all that we do. Today, consider how you can approach life with humility, seeking not personal recognition, but God's glory.

**Journal:** Reflect on the ways you approach daily life. Do you focus more on receiving recognition or on helping others succeed and glorifying God? What steps can you take to shift your mindset and actions to better align with the example of Jesus, ensuring that God receives the glory in all you do?

**One-sentence prayer:** Heavenly Father, help me point others to You today, giving You all the glory.

*Further hope and encouragement: John 4:27-35*

# DAY 97
# Owning or Blaming?

*"You hypocrite, first take the plank out of your own eye, and then you will see clearly to remove the speck from your brother's eye."*
*Matthew 7:5*

I'm embarrassed to share the story in today's devotion, but I'm going to do it anyway because I believe it holds an important lesson. My family and I were on our annual trip to Cape May, New Jersey, in June, after another school year wrapped up. Time on the beach, great food, lots of sun, and no school–sounds perfect, right? However, the trip wasn't going as planned, and we were struggling as a family. Finally, one morning, I gathered the family for a "team meeting" on the sidewalk in Cape May. I can still picture Carly and three kids looking up at me. Like any "great" leader, I declared, "Here's what we're going to do. We're going to go around the circle and say how each one of us has played a role in making this trip not go well." Oh, what a mistake. I can still see the look on Carly's face, as if she was silently thinking, "You're an idiot." I ended up putting everyone on the spot, accusing them of making the trip miserable, and it was all because of my poor attitude. My grumpiness clouded my judgment, and I tried to deflect blame onto others, which, in reality, was the last thing I should have done.

Jesus taught us to take ownership, especially when things go wrong. In Matthew 7:5, Jesus says, "You hypocrite, first take the plank out of your own eye, and then you will see clearly to remove the speck from your brother's eye." This verse emphasizes the importance of self-reflection and humility before pointing out the faults in others. It calls us to take responsibility for our own actions and shortcomings before addressing the issues of those around us. We are all human, and when things aren't going well, it's easy to blame others, but often, we need to pause and ask ourselves how we may be contributing to the situation. Taking ownership of our mistakes helps us grow and brings clarity to situations where we might otherwise be blind to our own role.

**Journal:** Reflect on a time when you tried to shift blame onto others rather than taking ownership of the situation. How did that impact your relationships or the outcome? How can you do better in the future when faced with challenges, ensuring that you take responsibility and approach situations with humility?

**One-sentence prayer:** Heavenly Father, help me to take ownership of my actions, learning from them, and reflecting your grace in every situation.

***Further hope and encouragement: Matthew 7:1-6***

# DAY 98
# Functioning Burnout

*What good is it for someone to gain the whole world, yet forfeit their soul?*
*Mark 8:36*

Hi, I'm Zac Bauermaster, and I'm a recovering functioning burnout. While I've never struggled with alcohol, I battled a different addiction: the constant chase for more—more approval, more accomplishments, more control, more "what's next." At my lowest, I was stuck in a cycle of striving and crashing, chasing the next thing to feel fulfilled. I've made progress, but I know how easy it is to slip back if I'm not intentional about anchoring my life in God's presence and purpose. In those seasons, I lost sight of who I was—and Whose I was. I focused on success, recognition, and productivity while neglecting the roots that sustain me: my spiritual health and connection with God. That pursuit left me exhausted, overwhelmed, and anxious.

Striving doesn't always look like chasing big goals. Sometimes it's the everyday grind—trying to keep a clean home in chaos, seeking peace through control, or scrolling for affirmation. It might be trying to keep everyone happy or finally feeling like we belong. But God doesn't call us to fit in—He calls us to belong to Him. A few years ago, I met Tony Dungy, whose humility and faith deeply inspire me. He signs every book with Mark 8:36, reminding us that worldly success means nothing if it costs our souls. The first step to healing is recognizing when we're off course and asking for help. The Holy Spirit isn't just near—He's here, ready to meet us in our weariness and lead us back to peace and purpose. Romans 8:26 says, "The Spirit helps us in our weakness... interceding for us with groans that words cannot express." So here's the challenge: Are we chasing what truly matters, or are we stuck in the cycle of striving? Let today be a reset. Let's choose to live for what lasts.

**Journal:** What are the moments or mindsets that trigger your striving? How might you root yourself in God's presence and purpose when those moments arise?

**One-sentence prayer:** Heavenly Father, help me trade busyness for fruitfulness and glorify You in how I live each day.

***Further hope and encouragement: Mark 8:34-38***

# DAY 99
# Pause and Take a Deep Breath

*In the beginning God created the heavens and the earth.*
*Genesis 1:1*

Take a moment to pause and breathe deeply. Let go of the stress you've been carrying, and focus on exhaling slowly. If you need to take more deep breaths—do it. As you breathe out, notice your shoulders drop. We often don't realize how tense we are until we consciously release it. Today, make it a point to slow down in all areas of your life and be more aware of the world around you. Remember, God is the Creator, and we are His creation.

We often rush through life so quickly that we forget to pause, rest, and appreciate God's handiwork. The pressure builds, and we risk becoming like an overfilled balloon, ready to burst. It's crucial for us to intentionally deflate that stress with moments of stillness. As we walk or drive today, let's take in the beauty of what's around us. Let's go outside and pause to admire the beauty and intricacies of a tree. Let's look at the people in our lives and remember that they, too, are part of God's creation. We are uniquely made by God, as is everything and everyone we encounter. Psalm 104:33 says, "I will sing to the Lord all my life; I will sing praise to my God as long as I live." Let's enjoy the beauty of His creation today, and allow it to remind us of the Creator's greatness. It will give us a fresh perspective for the day ahead.

**Journal:** What stress are you holding onto today? Pause and reflect on how you can slow down to experience the beauty of God's creation around you. How can you invite His peace into your busyness?

**One-sentence prayer:** Heavenly Father, help me slow down and see You in all of creation today

***Further hope and encouragement: Genesis 1***

# DAY 100
# I Just Wish It Was Easy

*Consider it pure joy, my brothers and sisters, whenever you face trials of many kinds, because you know that the testing of your faith produces perseverance. Let perseverance finish its work so that you may be mature and complete, not lacking anything.*
*James 1:2-4*

One cold December afternoon, I was putting up Christmas lights with my daughter, Eliot. If you've ever done this, you know how challenging it can be—tangled wires, burned-out bulbs, and frozen fingers. Here's a tip for those of us in colder climates: Don't wait until it's freezing to put up the Christmas lights. Despite the frustration, we kept a good sense of humor. At one point, as we struggled with a particularly difficult tree, Eliot looked at me and said, "Dad, I just wish this was easy." I chuckled and replied, "I know, me too. But when we're done, it will be worth it." As we continued, her words stayed with me. How often do I feel the same way in life? There are days when I silently think, I just wish it was easy. Have you ever felt that way? But life isn't meant to be easy. If it were, we wouldn't rely on God's strength.

Looking at the verse from James, we often want to skip ahead to the part where we are mature and complete. We long for the strength and peace that come with perseverance. But God knows that it's through the testing of our faith that perseverance is built. Without the struggles, we wouldn't have the endurance needed to grow into the people God intends us to be. The truth is, we've each been called for a specific purpose. The Bible is filled with examples of people whose paths were far from simple. Moses led the Israelites through the wilderness, facing complaints and doubt at every turn. Gideon, though initially reluctant, defeated the Midianites with only three hundred men, relying fully on God's strength. And Jesus, the ultimate example, endured rejection, betrayal, and unimaginable pain to fulfill His mission on earth. None of these individuals had an easy road, but they trusted God's purpose and leaned on His strength. As I reflected on my daughter's words, I realized that the struggle with those lights mirrored the reality of life—it's messy, it's hard, but it's worth it. Let's embrace the challenges today, trusting that God is with us, guiding us, and equipping us to shine His light in the world.

**Journal:** Think about a current challenge you're facing, something that has made you wish it was easier. How might God be using this difficulty to grow your faith or impact others? Take time to thank Him for walking with you through these hard moments.

**One-sentence prayer:** Heavenly Father, help me to trust You through the struggles today.

*Further hope and encouragement: James 1*

# DAY 101
# Train for Godliness

*Have nothing to do with godless myths and old wives' tales; rather, train yourself to be godly. For physical training is of some value, but godliness has value for all things, holding promise for both the present life and the life to come.*
1 Timothy 4:7-8

Working toward a goal takes effort and intentionality. Whether it's physical fitness, learning a new skill, or growing spiritually, the process requires discipline and focus. If not approached with intention, it's easy to let our goals slip away. We all know that physical fitness demands commitment—eating well, exercising, staying hydrated, and getting enough rest. These habits, if followed consistently, help us grow stronger and healthier. And if we don't do these things, we risk losing progress, feeling drained, or even going backward in our health.

The same applies to our spiritual growth—if we don't make time for God, we can easily grow distant from Him. Just as physical training demands consistency, so does our walk with God. This involves dedicating ourselves to developing a deeper relationship with Him—spending time in His Word, praying, and engaging with a community of believers. It also means examining the desires of our heart and making sure they align with what matters most. Too often, we pour our time, energy, and resources into pursuits that are temporary, forgetting the value of spiritual growth. Training ourselves for godliness means choosing to prioritize the eternal over the fleeting. It requires daily commitments that strengthen our faith and deepen our dependence on God—transforming us to reflect His character in everything we do. It's time to work out. Let's train ourselves for godliness today.

**Journal:** What areas of your life reveal a lack of intentionality in pursuing godliness? How can you adjust your habits this week to grow closer to God and reflect His character in your everyday life?

**One-sentence prayer:** Heavenly Father, I want to grow in You.

*Further hope and encouragement: 1 Timothy 4*

# DAY 102
# Show Me the Way

*Let the morning bring me word of your unfailing love, for I have put my trust in you. Show me the way I should go, for to you I entrust my life.*
Psalm 143:8

Every morning, I pour myself a cup of coffee. Most days, Carly or I prepare the coffee maker the night before and set the timer so it's ready when we walk into the kitchen. I reach into the cupboard, grab an empty mug, and fill it to the brim with what was, just moments before, an empty cup. I don't know where you find yourself today. Maybe you feel like that empty mug—tired, worn down, and longing to be filled. Or perhaps you're brimming with energy, ready to pour into others.

In many ways, we're all like that empty coffee mug, and God's Word is the coffee. Each day, we must allow ourselves to be filled first—knowing God more, understanding ourselves in light of who He is, and discerning what He's calling us to do. David Mathis puts it this way: "We go on the offensive when we feed our souls in some regular rhythm before the events and tasks and disappointments of daily life begin streaming our way." Just as adults on a plane are instructed to secure their own oxygen masks before assisting others, we need to create space for God to fill us through His Word so we can live, love, and serve others with strength and purpose. Quiet time with Jesus isn't just a good idea—it's a necessity. God already knows what's coming your way today, and His Word is your guide to navigate it. There's no substitute for starting your day with Him. Take the time today to let God fill you, so you can walk in His strength and pour into the world around you with His grace. Let God show you the way today.

**Journal:** Are you taking time each day to let God fill you? If not, what small adjustments can you make to prioritize quiet time with Him? How might being filled by God's Word impact how you lead and serve others?

**One-sentence prayer:** Heavenly Father, show me the way to go today.

***Further hope and encouragement: Psalm 143***

# DAY 103
# Prayer

*Pray continually.*
*1 Thessalonians 5:17*

Pour your heart out to God in prayer today. God doesn't desire a perfect prayer; He desires your heart. If you're struggling with where to start in prayer, try the **ACTS** model by aligning your prayer as follows: **A**doration, **C**onfession, **T**hanksgiving, and **S**upplication. Pray with me today:

Heavenly Father,
You are Almighty God,
Creator of the heavens and the earth.
You are the beginning,
You are the end.
I humbly confess that I am nothing without You.
You cause my heart to beat,
You fill my lungs with air.
I can't take a step without You,
I can't speak without You.
I give You thanks.
Every good and perfect gift is from above.
Thank You for the gift of life.
Thank You for the gift of leadership.
Thank You for the gift of Jesus.
Guide and direct me to love like Jesus.
Strengthen me to lead like Jesus.
Help me be Your hands and Your feet,
Reflecting You in all I do today.
In Jesus' name, I pray, Amen.

**Journal:** Take a moment to reflect on your prayer life. Are there areas where you struggle to pray continually? Write about how you can incorporate more moments of prayer throughout your day. Use the **ACTS** model as a guide, and jot down a simple prayer using each of its components.

**One-sentence prayer:** Heavenly Father, You're all I want, You're all I need.

***Further hope and encouragement: Matthew 6:9-13***

## DAY 104
# Fruitful Living

*This is to my Father's glory, that you bear much fruit,*
*showing yourselves to be my disciples.*
*John 15:8*

One of my favorite quotes used to be: "Leadership is influence, nothing more, nothing less." I still believe there's truth in that statement, but over time, my perspective has shifted. Influence is powerful—but it's not the ultimate goal. And here's the thing: we're all leaders. Whether it's in our homes, workplaces, schools, or neighborhoods, each of us has influence right where we are. But as followers of Jesus, we're not called to simply influence others; we're called to live fruitfully—for God's glory, not our own.

Fruitfulness reframes the purpose of our influence. It moves the spotlight from ourselves to the impact God can make through us. A fruitful life isn't measured by likes, followers, or recognition, but by the lasting seeds we plant in others through love, kindness, truth, and grace. And here's the key: we can't bear fruit on our own. In John 15:4, Jesus reminds us that a branch cannot bear fruit unless it remains connected to the vine. That connection—our daily abiding in Him—is what gives life to our influence. True influence flows from fruitfulness, not the other way around. The more we stay rooted in Christ, the more our lives overflow with purpose and impact. Fruit carries seeds, and God often uses even the smallest seeds we leave behind to grow something far greater than we could imagine. Jesus doesn't call us to temporary influence but to bear "fruit that will last" (John 15:16). That's what it means to live with eternity in mind.

**Journal:** Reflect on your daily life—are there areas where you're striving for influence over fruitfulness? What simple changes can help you stay more deeply connected to Jesus and allow Him to shape lasting impact through you?

**One-sentence prayer:** Heavenly Father, You're all I want, You're all I need—help me abide in You and bear fruit that lasts.

***Further hope and encouragement: John 15:1-17***

# DAY 105

# Love God and Love People

*Jesus replied: "'Love the Lord your God with all your heart and with all your soul and with all your mind.' This is the first and greatest commandment. And the second is like it: 'Love your neighbor as yourself.'"*
*Matthew 22:37-39*

What's on your to-do list today? I'm sure there's a lot to get done! Life can feel overwhelming at times, and we often overcomplicate things. I remember talking to a mentor of mine about an upcoming day. I shared everything on my calendar and to-do list—a long list of what I believed I needed to accomplish. He listened, then looked at me and said, "Zac, you certainly have a lot to do today. It sounds complicated. I want to encourage you to keep it simple and write these five words at the top of a notebook each day: "Love God and love people." Since that day, I've made it a habit to remind myself daily to keep it simple. That simple reminder helps me refocus on what truly matters: loving God and loving people.

When Jesus was asked which commandment was the greatest, He replied: "Love the Lord your God with all your heart and with all your soul and with all your mind. This is the first and greatest commandment. And the second is like it: 'Love your neighbor as yourself'" (Matthew 22:37-39). Here's the thing—we can't truly love others if we are not first loving God with all our heart, soul, and mind. Our relationship with Him shapes how we interact with the world. When we prioritize loving God and loving people, we not only simplify our to-do lists, but we also bring more meaning, peace, and purpose to each day. No matter what's on your schedule today, keep it simple: Love God and love people.

**Journal:** As you look at your to-do list today, remember the advice to "keep it simple." How can you focus on loving God and loving people in each task? Reflect on how prioritizing these two principles can bring clarity and purpose to your day.

**One-sentence prayer:** Heavenly Father, help me keep it simple today, loving You and others every step of the way.

***Further hope and encouragement: Matthew 22:34-40***

# DAY 106
# Bite Your Tongue

*Do not let any unwholesome talk come out of your mouths,*
*but only what is helpful for building others up according to*
*their needs, that it may benefit those who listen.*
*Ephesians 4:29*

My parents always challenged me to be slow with my words—encouraging me to pause, think before speaking, and pay closer attention to the things that come out of my mouth. That challenge began in our house, especially with how I talked to my sisters. As the instigating middle child, I didn't always use the best choice of words. I could be quick with a comeback or stir the pot just to get a reaction. But my parents didn't let those moments slide. They would give me a good breath mint to help take care of the stink that came out of my mouth: a bar of soap. More importantly, they asked a simple but convicting question: Are your words building others up and benefiting them—or tearing them down? It's a question we often pose to kids, but the truth is, we need it just as much as adults. That challenge reshaped how I communicate, especially when I'm talking about people who aren't present.

Imagine if a recording of every conversation you've had was played back publicly. How would you feel? More importantly, how would those you talked about feel? It's a humbling thought, but one that can guide us toward greater wisdom and care in our conversations. Words are powerful. They can bring life or do damage. Paul reminds us in Ephesians 4:29 not to let any unwholesome talk come out of our mouths, but only what is helpful for building others up. James 3 compares the tongue to a ship's rudder or a tiny spark—small in size, yet capable of steering lives or setting things ablaze. Our words matter. They can carry peace or create chaos. So today, let's commit to guarding our speech. Let's use our words to encourage, to express gratitude, to speak truth with kindness. And when negativity tempts us, let's bite our tongues and choose grace instead.

**Journal:** When are you most tempted to speak carelessly or negatively about others? What practices could help you speak more intentionally and reflect God's love in your conversations?

**One-sentence prayer:** Heavenly Father, help me use my words to build up, not tear down—let them reflect Your heart in every conversation.

**Further hope and encouragement: Ephesians 4:25-32**

# DAY 107
# Prayer Partners

*For where two or three come together in my name, there I am with them.*
*Matthew 18:20*

We weren't meant to navigate life alone. God created us for community, and that truth holds steady no matter our stage of life or circumstances. When we walk through seasons of challenge or joy, having someone to pray with and for makes a powerful difference. As Jesus reminds us in Matthew 18:20, "For where two or three come together in my name, there am I with them." Prayer partners—those we can count on for encouragement, support, and prayer—help anchor us in God's presence. If we don't already have someone in our lives to walk with us in this way, we can ask God to place the right person on our hearts. Together, we can build one another up, carry each other's burdens, and reflect Christ's love more fully.

When we journey alongside a prayer partner, we deepen not only our connection with each other but also our relationship with God. We grow together in faith, keep each other accountable, and celebrate answered prayers with joy. Jesus modeled the value of spiritual companionship when He sent His disciples out in pairs. In the same way, we thrive when we have others beside us, praying through life's ups and downs, lifting each other's needs, and reminding one another of God's promises. We were never meant to go it alone—God's presence meets us when we gather, even in the smallest of groups. Together, let's be a people who pray boldly, support one another, and live out our faith in community.

**Journal:** Who might God be placing on your heart to partner with in prayer?

**One-sentence prayer:** Heavenly Father, lead me to prayer partners who will walk beside me in faith and lift me up in Your love.

***Further hope and encouragement: Matthew 18:15-20***

## DAY 108
# Setting Priorities

*For where your treasure is, there your heart will be also.*
*Matthew 6:21*

In life, it's easy to get caught up in the demands of daily responsibilities—work tasks, family commitments, personal passions, and community obligations. The challenge often lies in knowing where to direct your attention and energy. I've found that when I struggle to prioritize the right things in the right order, life becomes chaotic—rushing from one task to the next, always in a hurry. But when I make Jesus my number one priority, everything else starts to fall into place. There's a deep peace that comes from remembering that my ultimate purpose is to live with Jesus at the center. Life becomes more focused and intentional when our priorities are aligned with Him. Are you currently experiencing calm or chaos when it comes to your priorities?

Just as David declared in Psalm 23:1, "The Lord is my Shepherd," we are all called to follow the Good Shepherd in every area of our lives. When we put Jesus first, He leads us through the complexities of life with clarity and wisdom. Our families, friendships, workplaces, and communities are all impacted when we live from a place of peace that only comes from keeping Him at the center. We must be intentional about how we set our priorities, making space for what truly matters. What treasures are we chasing right now? Are they aligned with God's calling for us to live with integrity, compassion, and purpose? Prioritizing Jesus doesn't just benefit us—it blesses everyone around us. So let's reflect today: What priorities do we need to realign to ensure Jesus is truly at the center of our lives?

**Journal:** What priorities feel out of balance in your life right now? How can you adjust your schedule or mindset to put Jesus first and allow Him to guide your steps?

**One-sentence prayer:** Heavenly Father, help me to set my priorities with You at the center.

***Further hope and encouragement: Matthew 6***

## DAY 109
# Renew Your Strength

*but those who hope in the Lord will renew their strength.*
*They will soar on wings like eagles; they will run and not*
*grow weary, they will walk and not be faint.*
Isaiah 40:31

"I think I'm done." The text message caught me off guard. Unsure of what he meant, I followed up: "Done with what?" His response came quickly: "Education. How much have you considered working outside of education?" Of course, that wasn't a conversation for text, so we made time to meet. When we sat down together, he admitted, "I've lost my strength. What once felt like a calling now feels like a burden. I don't know if I can do it much longer." Honestly, I was both shocked and not surprised. This was a positive, energetic leader who always loved his work in education. Yet the relentless demands of his job had worn him down. He's not alone.

So, where do we turn when our strength is slipping away? Where are we looking for hope and renewal? If you're like me, when difficulties rise—whether at home or at work—it's easy to lose sight of the everlasting God, the Creator of the ends of the earth. We get tired. We stumble. We fall. We're ready to give up at times. Yet Isaiah 40 reminds us that God does not grow weary. Instead, He gives strength to the weary (Isaiah 40:29) and offers us a promise: "Those who hope in the Lord will renew their strength. They will soar on wings like eagles; they will run and not grow weary, they will walk and not be faint." This doesn't mean that work, responsibilities, or struggles will suddenly become easier, but it does mean we don't have to carry the load alone. If you're feeling done, questioning your calling or purpose—whether in your career, family, or other areas of life—turn to Him today and don't give up. Renew your strength in the Lord.

**Journal:** Reflect on a time when you thought, "I think I'm done." How did God provide strength during that season? Consider how His presence reminded you that your story wasn't over, and identify specific steps you can take to seek His strength and guidance if you face a similar challenge again.

**One-sentence prayer:** Heavenly Father, renew my strength.

***Further hope and encouragement: Isaiah 40***

## DAY 110
# Quiet Waters

*He leads me beside quiet waters.*
*Psalm 23:2*

When I was serving as an assistant principal, I had a forty-five-minute commute to work each day. I often felt anxious during the drive—not because I didn't want to go to work, but because I was restless about the time I couldn't be productive. Those forty-five minutes felt like a loss of control. I wasn't getting anything done, and it left me uneasy. Maybe you can relate. Many of us feel more anxious when we're not working than when we are. Staying busy gives us a sense of control, but when we're forced to slow down, it can feel unsettling. That restless feeling began to shift when I noticed something along my commute. About ten minutes from the school, I passed a large pond tucked beneath weeping willow trees. On many mornings, the rising sun reflected beautifully off the water, with white ducks floating peacefully on the surface and fog lifting gently from the stillness.

One morning, as I took in the scene, I was reminded of Psalm 23:2: "He leads me beside quiet waters." Those quiet waters are where He restores our souls. I realized I needed to shift my mindset from trusting in my own effort to trusting in Him. Over time, that daily drive became a sacred space. Each day as I approached the pond, I began to pause, take a deep breath, and recite that verse: "He leads me beside quiet waters." Instead of clinging to the need to be in control, I rested in the truth—and thanked God—that I wasn't the one in control. I didn't know what challenges the day would hold, but God began to calm my restless heart as I allowed Him to lead me into stillness in His presence. We all face moments when life feels overwhelming or out of sync. But in the midst of the chaos—or even in the quiet—whether at home, at work, or in our own minds, God invites us to slow down and rest with Him. Despite the noise around us today, may we follow God and allow Him to lead us to the quiet waters.

**Journal:** Consider a time when you felt restless or unsettled. How might God be calling you to slow down and trust Him more fully? What "quiet waters" can you intentionally seek today to allow Him to restore your soul?

**One-sentence prayer:** Heavenly Father, lead me to the still waters today, and help me rest in You.

***Further hope and encouragement: Psalm 23***

# DAY 111
# Overflow

*Come to me, all you who are weary and burdened, and I will give you rest. Take my yoke upon you and learn from me, for I am gentle and humble in heart, and you will find rest for your souls. For my yoke is easy and my burden is light.*
*Matthew 11:28-30*

I struggle with asthma. As a kid, I had it, then it disappeared for most of my life—until it came back in full force when I was thirty-seven. It was scary. I didn't know what was happening, but I knew one thing: I couldn't breathe. If you're not familiar with blood oxygen levels, the ideal range is 97-100. When my asthma flares up, my oxygen levels drop to 85-88, which is dangerously low. I learned something important about myself: my oxygen typically maxes out at 95. That's fine under normal conditions, but if it drops even a little—to the low 90s—I struggle to breathe. And guess what? Over five months, I spent eight nights in the hospital because I wasn't getting enough oxygen. When that happened, I couldn't help anyone—not my family, my friends, or my colleagues.

The same is true for our emotional, mental, and spiritual well-being. Too often, we run on empty, letting our energy drain to dangerously low levels before trying to refill with a weekend off or a vacation. But just like oxygen, we need consistent care to stay healthy—not just emergency refills when we're already depleted. Instead of waiting until we're burned out, we should be maintaining a healthy rhythm, keeping our tanks full so we have something to give. When we operate from overflow, we're able to pour into others without completely draining ourselves. Whether at home, work, or wherever we serve, the people around us need us at our best—not gasping for breath while trying to help them. Matthew 11:28-30 reminds us, "Come to me, all you who are weary and burdened, and I will give you rest. Take my yoke upon you and learn from me, for I am gentle and humble in heart, and you will find rest for your souls. For my yoke is easy and my burden is light." Begin with resting in Jesus, and just as Jesus offers rest and renewal, we, too, need to take time to replenish ourselves so we can serve from a place of overflow rather than exhaustion.

**Journal:** What are three things that restore and refresh you? How can you make them a regular part of your routine so you are consistently operating from overflow?

**One-sentence prayer:** Heavenly Father, help me to care for myself in a way that allows me to serve others with energy, joy, and love.

***Further hope and encouragement: Mark 6:30-32***

# DAY 112

# Give Everything You Have...
# and Watch What Happens

*Here is a boy with five small barley loaves and two small fish,*
*but how far will they go among so many?*
*John 6:9*

I once met a man who didn't have much—by the world's standards, his situation seemed hopeless. But his motto stuck with me: "I may not have it all, but I'm going to give it my all, each and every day." Wow. That powerful mindset reminds me of the story of Jesus feeding the five thousand. When a massive, hungry crowd gathered, the disciples didn't know how they could possibly feed everyone. Then they noticed a boy with five small loaves and two fish (John 6:9). Andrew, one of the disciples, pointed out the offering—but added skeptically, "But how far will they go among so many?"

Maybe that's how you feel right now. You're facing a crowd of challenges with what seems like limited time, energy, or resources—your own "five loaves and two fish." You might feel like it's not enough. But here's the truth: you don't need to have it all. If you're a son or daughter of the King, you already have access to what you need for today. Some days it might not feel like much, but if you keep showing up and offering what you have, God will meet you there. That doesn't mean it will always be easy or comfortable, but that's exactly where God wants us to be—clinging to His strength. And just like in the story, He won't just meet the need—He'll go above and beyond. "When they had all had enough to eat, he (Jesus) said to his disciples, 'Gather the pieces that are left over'" (v.12). Not only did God provide—there was more than enough. So keep going. Give your all, right where you are, and trust God to multiply it. He is always faithful.

**Journal:** What "five loaves and two fish" can you offer today? Reflect on how you can start right where you are, using what you already have, and trust God to do the rest.

**One-sentence prayer:** Heavenly Father, help me to give my all each day, trusting You to take what I offer and multiply it for Your glory.

*Further hope and encouragement: John 6:1-14*

# DAY 113
# Only Jesus

*Now swear to me by the Lord that you will not cut off my descendants or wipe out my name from my father's family.*
*1 Samuel 24:21*

I was asked in an interview once, "What do you want your legacy to be?" I share this often, but we are called to be ambassadors for Christ—representing Jesus in all that we do, say, and think. As I write this morning, I feel convicted, realizing that I often go through the day representing myself and my "kingdom," rather than God and His. As much as I'd like to think I'm like David, "a man after God's own heart," I often find parallels with King Saul.

When Saul realized the kingdom of Israel would no longer be his and that David would be crowned king, he said to David, "Now swear to me that you will not cut off my descendants or wipe out my name from my father's family" (1 Samuel 24:21). Earlier, when Saul admitted his wrongdoing, he pleaded, "I have sinned, but please honor me before the elders of my people and before Israel" (1 Samuel 15:30). Let's break that down:

+ "Don't wipe out my name."
+ "Please honor me."

Saul became obsessed with self—his image, his legacy, and building a kingdom around his name. We see this in his repeated use of "my" and "me." So, back to that interview question: "What do you want your legacy to be?" Let's take the response beautifully expressed in the Casting Crowns (2018) song *Only Jesus*: "I don't want to leave a legacy. I don't care if they remember me—only Jesus."

**Journal:** Reflect on how you represent Jesus in your daily life. Are there moments when you focus more on building your own kingdom rather than God's? How can you shift your focus to leave a legacy that points to Him?

**One-sentence prayer:** Heavenly Father, it's all about You.

***Further hope and encouragement: 1 Samuel 24, Psalm 103***

## DAY 114

# Well Done, Good and Faithful Servant

*His master replied, "Well done, good and faithful servant!*
*You have been faithful with a few things; I will put you in charge of*
*many things. Come and share your master's happiness!"*
*Matthew 25:21*

When it comes to the Five Love Languages (Chapman, 2015), I'm a words-of-affirmation kind of person. I'm deeply encouraged by the words of others. When I empty the dishwasher, I patiently wait for Carly to say, "Well done, Zac; thank you so much!" Instead, she usually reminds me not to put the dishes away when they're still wet. Sometimes I will let her know that I emptied the dishwasher and she says, "Do you want me to throw you a parade or something?" Yes, actually I would like a parade. All joking aside, when someone lifts me up with their words, it motivates me to keep going. And not much beats hearing someone say, "Well done, I'm proud of you."

In the Parable of the Talents, Jesus tells the story of a man who goes away and entrusts his property to his servants. To each servant, the man gave talents of money according to their ability: five talents to one, two to another, and one to the third. The servants who received the five talents and the two talents immediately put the money to work, each doubling the talents they'd been given. When the master returned, the two men brought back the talents they had doubled. The master responded, "Well done, good and faithful servant! You have been faithful with a few things; I will put you in charge of many things" (Matthew 25:23). In life, God has entrusted us with various gifts, responsibilities, and opportunities. Like the two servants who "went at once," we are called to use what He has given us to make a difference in His kingdom. We should live each day knowing we are working for the Lord, to one day hear Him say, "Well done, good and faithful servant."

**Journal:** What talents, gifts, or responsibilities has God entrusted to you? How can you faithfully steward them this week to make an eternal impact, rather than focusing on earthly recognition?

**One-sentence prayer:** Heavenly Father, thank You for the gifts and opportunities You've given me in life.

*Further hope and encouragement: Matthew 25:14-30*

# DAY 115
# Don't Hide Your Talents

*"So I was afraid and went out and hid your talent in the ground.
See, here is what belongs to you."*
Matthew 25:25

In the Parable of the Talents, we see two servants who immediately take the talents they've been given and put them to work, doubling them for their master. However, the third servant, who was given one talent according to his ability, chose a different path. Instead of using it, he "went off, dug a hole in the ground and hid his master's money" (v.18). When his master returned, the servant explained his reasoning: "I was afraid and went out and hid your talent in the ground" (v.25). His fear led him to inaction, and in doing so, he missed the opportunity to grow what had been entrusted to him.

Here's the thing: We are often like the third servant. God has equipped each of us with unique gifts to use for His glory, yet fear and self-doubt can paralyze us, keeping us from stepping out in faith. Fear can shrink our vision and limit our God-given potential, but we're called to live boldly, trusting that God will supply everything we need. Scripture reminds us in 2 Timothy 1:7, "For God did not give us a spirit of timidity, but a spirit of power, of love, and of self-discipline." Additionally, 1 Peter 4:10 encourages us: "Each one should use whatever gift he has received to serve others, faithfully administering God's grace in its various forms." Let's stop hiding, step outside of our comfort zones, and move forward with humble confidence, remembering that we are ambassadors for Christ in His Kingdom. Don't hide your talents.

**Journal:** What is one area in your life where fear or self-doubt has kept you from taking action, and what step of faith can you take this week to use your God-given talents?

**One-sentence prayer:** Heavenly Father, help me to move beyond fear and inaction, trusting You to guide and equip me as I step out in faith.

***Further hope and encouragement: Matthew 25:14-30, 1 Peter 4***

## DAY 116
# Who is the Greatest?

*Then he (Jesus) said to them, "Whoever welcomes this little child*
*in my name welcomes me; and whoever welcomes me welcomes the*
*one who sent me. For he who is least among you all—he is the greatest."*
*Luke 9:48*

In sports, we often hear conversations about who is the GOAT—the greatest of all time. Whether it's Michael Jordan, Tom Brady, Serena Williams, Usain Bolt, Lionel Messi, or Roger Federer, there are countless people and sports shows that spend time debating it. Now imagine sitting at a table with Jesus and a group of people discussing their accomplishments. As you're sitting there, an argument breaks out about who is the greatest. This story from Luke absolutely amazes me—until I humbly recognize that I'm more like the disciples in this conversation than I'd like to admit. The disciples, chosen by Jesus, found themselves debating their own greatness—even in His presence! Are you kidding me? Yet, if we're honest, we've all been there. Pride has a sneaky way of camouflaging itself within us, even as we strive to serve others.

This story is a humbling reminder that true greatness in God's eyes is found in humility. Jesus, the greatest to ever walk this earth, responds to the disciples' argument with these powerful words: "For he who is least among you all—he is the greatest" (Luke 9:48). This response is completely counter to what the world teaches about success. But as followers of Jesus, we are called to be "meek and lowly of heart" (Matthew 11:29) and to make ourselves of no reputation (Philippians 2:7). True greatness isn't about recognition or self-promotion. It's not about being the greatest. It's about taking the lowest place, considering others better than ourselves, and serving with a humble heart. That's humility. That's true greatness. That's Jesus. Follow Him—He is the greatest.

**Journal:** Reflect on a time when pride influenced your actions or decisions. How might you practice humility in your daily life today, this week, and moving forward?

**One-sentence prayer:** Heavenly Father, help me follow Jesus' example of living with humility.

***Further hope and encouragement: Luke 9***

# DAY 117
# Reap What You Sow

*Let us not become weary in doing good, for at the proper*
*time we will reap a harvest if we do not give up.*
*Galatians 6:9*

My oldest daughter and I headed to the school to practice basketball. It was about three weeks from her first junior high basketball try-out. As a principal's kid, she loved having access to the gym. The practice started out well—we did some shooting and layups. Then, she wanted to practice her left-handed layups. As she began, I noticed tears welling up in her eyes. Before I knew it, she was sitting on a basketball underneath the hoop, leaning against the wall. She was frustrated—not with me, but with herself. She said, "I'm mad at myself. I didn't practice like I should have to improve for the season. I don't feel prepared for the tryout." As I listened, I thought to myself: "Oh, how many times have I been exactly where she is?" Whether it's eating well, working out, reading, writing, spending time in God's Word, praying, or investing in my relationships, I've fallen short more times than I can count. I'm not always disciplined in the small, daily moments, and then suddenly, a big moment comes along, and I feel unprepared.

Life requires preparation, and there are no disciplines more important than the spiritual ones that shape how we live each day. Are we faithfully doing the small things that lead to fruitful outcomes, or do we allow distractions to take our time, leaving us unprepared for what lies ahead? It's not easy, but we are encouraged to not become weary in doing good, for at the proper time we will reap a harvest if we do not give up (Galatians 6:9). Consistent preparation and disciplined actions honor God and equip us to serve Him and others with excellence. Faithfulness in both the small and big tasks matters—it's the seeds we plant today that will grow into tomorrow's harvest. As Proverbs 4:23 reminds us, "Above all else, guard your heart, for everything you do flows from it." By nurturing our hearts through spiritual disciplines, we align ourselves with God's purpose, ensuring that our actions stem from a wellspring of devotion and integrity. We reap what we sow.

**Journal:** What seeds are you planting in your daily life? Are there areas where you feel unprepared because of a lack of discipline? Reflect on one small step you can take today to sow seeds that will lead to a harvest in the future.

**One-sentence prayer:** Heavenly Father, help me to be faithful in the small moments and trust Your perfect timing.

***Further hope and encouragement: Galatians 6***

# DAY 118
# Live As a Light

*When Jesus spoke again to the people, he said, "I am the light of the world. Whoever follows me will never walk in darkness, but will have the light of life."*
*John 8:12*

We are called to be a light in this world. While we are not the Light ourselves, we are lit by the Light of the world—Jesus. Growing up, I memorized Psalm 119:105: "Your word is a lamp to my feet and a light for my path." When do we need a lamp to see the path ahead? When it's dark. And though we don't always live as if this is true, the reality is that darkness surrounds us every day. We desperately need God's Word to be our guiding light. We want to be in His Word—first listening well to it, but not stopping there. We must also put it into practice (Luke 8:21).

As we seek to live as a light by living out the Word, the first step is acknowledging that there is nothing special about us—what is special is Christ in us. We don't want to hide that light; we must let it shine. Jesus tells us that we are the light of the world (Matthew 5:14) and calls us to let our light shine before others (Matthew 5:16). When people see the way you live, do they stop and think, "Something is different about him or her"? Our purpose is to follow the Light of the world so that we do not walk in darkness but instead carry the light of life (John 8:12) into the lives of others. Do the people around you see Jesus—the Light of the world—in you? It's a dark world out there—live as a light today.

**Journal:** Who is someone in your life that radiates the light of Christ? In what areas of your life do you struggle to shine Christ's light? How can you be more intentional about reflecting His love and truth to those around you?

**One-sentence prayer:** Heavenly Father, You are the Light of the world.

***Further hope and encouragement: Matthew 5:14-18***

# DAY 119
# Guilt (less)

*But God demonstrates his own love for us in this: while*
*we were still sinners Christ died for us.*
Romans 5:8

Do you ever wake up in the morning and feel weighed down by guilt? In the stillness of the early hours, are you flooded with regret over something you said or did? Guilt over how you treated others? As I write today's devotion, that's exactly where I find myself. After a busy stretch recently, I was tired, and my heart was exposed. Can you guess who bore the brunt of it? My kids. Why? Because they weren't doing what I wanted them to do, listening the way I wanted them to listen, or showing the respect I thought they should. And what did I do? I raised my voice several times throughout the day, saying things like:

+ "How many times do I have to tell you?!"
+ "You've got to start listening. You have to do better."
+ "I shouldn't have to repeat myself so many times!"

Maybe you've been there, too—whether at home in your personal life or in your professional life. As I prayed and asked for forgiveness, I was overwhelmed by the realization of what a gracious and merciful God we serve. Despite the fact that I mess up and fall short every day, He doesn't respond to me the way I responded to my kids. God doesn't say, "Zac, how many times do I have to tell you? You need to start listening. You've got to do better. I shouldn't have to repeat myself so many times." Instead, He reminds me of His love and grace day after day, moment after moment. He sent His Son, Jesus, to die on the cross for you and me. Because of that, we are washed white as snow. As Romans 5:8 says, "But God demonstrates his own love for us in this: While we were still sinners, Christ died for us." So, rest in these two truths today:

1. If you are feeling guilty or like you're constantly falling short, pour out your heart to God. You don't have to carry the guilt because of what Jesus did on the cross.

2. Check your heart. Are you extending Christ's love, grace, and mercy to others?

Because of Jesus, and Jesus alone, you aren't guilty—you are guiltless.

**Journal:** What guilt do you need to release to God today? How can you overflow His love and grace to others?

**One-sentence prayer:** Lord, thank You for Your love and grace that frees me from guilt and allows me to walk in Your mercy.

*Further hope and encouragement: Romans 5*

# DAY 120
# Everyone is Looking for You

*Simon and his companions went to look for him, and when
they found him, they exclaimed: "Everyone is looking for you!"*
*Mark 1:36-37*

In Mark 1, as Jesus wakes up early to find a solitary place to pray, Simon and his companions go out looking for Him. When they find Him, they exclaim, "Everyone is looking for you!" (v. 37). This story reminds me of a couple of things. First, it reminds me of Carly and kids. She doesn't get much solitude because the kids are constantly gravitating toward her with needs and questions. Much like my kids wander through the house calling, "Mom, Mom, Mom" (while walking right past me), I can picture Simon and his friends walking around calling, "Jesus, Jesus, Jesus."

Secondly, I'm sure you've felt this in your own life—whether at home or at work. You try to grab a moment of solitude, just a few minutes of peace and quiet is all you need. Then, at that exact moment, a child or spouse comes looking for you. A phone call or text message arrives, and someone needs your help. Someone at work pops into your room or office to say, "Someone's looking for you." Some days, all you crave is silence; instead, someone greets you with, "Do you have a minute?" or "Can I talk to you?" There are days when it truly feels like *everyone* is looking for you. Next time that happens, instead of feeling frustrated, let's respond like Jesus and say, "That is why I've come" (Mark 1:38). God has given you responsibilities for His kingdom. When everyone's looking for you, don't hide—go and let your light shine. That's why you are exactly where you're supposed to be, with the people you're supposed to be with.

**Journal:** What responsibilities has God given you for His kingdom? How can you shine your light for the people around you today?

**One-sentence prayer:** Lord, thank You for placing me where I am. Help me embrace my responsibilities and shine Your light for others.

### Further hope and encouragement: Mark 1

## DAY 121
# Does It Help You Run?

*Therefore, since we are surrounded by such a great cloud of witnesses,
let us throw off everything that hinders and the sin that so easily entangles.
And let us run with perseverance the race marked out for us.*
*Hebrews 12:1*

It was a Monday morning when I headed out early for a three-mile run. I felt awful as I began running, and it only worsened with each step. Here's why: I was tired and hadn't slept well the night before. I didn't sleep well because I hadn't eaten well. Now, I'm not here to blame my mom, but every Sunday night my family enjoys a wonderful feast at my parents' house, and every Sunday night, I tend to overeat at my mom's buffet. This particular Sunday, I indulged in second and third portions of roast beef and mashed potatoes. Then, I ate freshly baked chocolate chip cookies like they were Tic Tacs, followed by a couple of bowls of ice cream. Was I done? Of course not. Then I searched the cupboards and found hidden candy.

Hebrews 12:1 tells us to "throw off everything that hinders and the sin that so easily entangles, and let us run with perseverance the race marked out for us." You are in a race right now—not a race to win first place, but a race of life that God has designed specifically for you. A race in which He has called you to specific tasks and people. Let me ask you this: Like my miserable three-mile run, which was hindered by my choices the night before, what's hindering you from running the race God has marked out for you? When I eat healthy and get good sleep, I am stronger and feel better during my runs. So ask yourself this question: Do your daily decisions help you run, or do they get in the way of living like Jesus?

**Journal:** Create a list of what you're doing when you're running your race well. Create another list of what you're doing when your race is hindered. What's one thing hindering you from running your race well? What's one small change you can make this week to help you move forward?

**One-sentence prayer:** Heavenly Father, help me fix my eyes on You to run the race You have marked out for me.

**Further hope and encouragement: Hebrews 12**

# DAY 122
# Day By Day

*So he asked Jesse, "Are these all the sons you have?" "There is still the youngest," Jesse answered. "He is tending the sheep." Samuel said, "Send for him; we will not sit down until he arrives."*
1 Samuel 16:11

I'm someone who is always looking ahead and can easily get caught up in what's next. Whether I'm exploring new opportunities or dreaming of what could be, I sometimes lose sight of the present. On top of that, I'm involved in so many things that there are times I feel like I'm just going through the motions—moving from one responsibility to the next—without fully being present in any of them. A superintendent once reminded me often, "Be where your feet are." You may have heard that phrase before, but have you ever truly stopped to reflect on it—and, more importantly, applied it? As I write today's devotion, I am sitting at my dining room table with my Bible open, my notebook beside me, and my devotional in front of me—my feet firmly planted on the floor. Yet, my mind has wandered elsewhere. It takes effort and intentionality to limit distractions and refocus on the moment.

One of my favorite stories in the Bible is when David was called to be the next king of Israel. He wasn't out campaigning for the role; instead, he was humbly tending the sheep when Samuel arrived at Jesse's house to anoint one of his sons as king. I can picture David's older brothers lined up, each hoping to be chosen. Even Samuel initially assumed Eliab was the one. But one by one, Jesse's seven sons passed before him, and the Lord had not chosen any of them. Samuel then asked, "Are these all the sons you have?" (v. 11). Jesse responded, "There is still the youngest, but he is tending the sheep." David remained faithful to the task before him. He was exactly where God had placed him in that moment—shepherding his flock. That's where his feet were. So today, don't look back, and don't get lost in what's ahead. Be faithful right where you are. God has placed you in this moment for a purpose. Walk in it, day by day.

**Journal:** In what areas of your life do you struggle to be present? How can you practice being faithful where your feet are today?

**One-sentence prayer:** Heavenly Father, help me to be present and faithful in the work You have called me to today.

***Further hope and encouragement: 1 Samuel 16***

## DAY 123
# Hiding in the Baggage

*And the Lord said, "Yes, he has hidden himself among the baggage."*
*1 Samuel 10:22*

Some days, I feel like hiding—I really do. Whether it's staying in bed a little longer to avoid facing the day, sitting in my car before walking into work, lingering in my office more than usual, or even delaying my walk into the house when I get home. If I'm being completely transparent, there are days when I would rather hide than face what's ahead. Maybe you even have a hiding spot from your kids! Don't get me wrong—I love what I do. I enjoy all of my roles. But that doesn't mean there aren't moments when the weight of responsibility feels overwhelming. I remember my first year of teaching, waking up in the middle of the night and loving the silence, unsure if I could face the next day. There have been days as a school leader and as a parent when I felt like I couldn't do it much longer. During one of those moments, Carly wisely reminded me, "God didn't call you because you were equipped for the job, but He will equip you for the job and provide you with everything you need."

After Saul was anointed king of Israel privately by Samuel, the time came for him to be presented publicly. Samuel gathered the tribes of Israel, but Saul was nowhere to be found. After searching for him, they discovered he was hiding among the baggage (1 Samuel 10:22). Saul was afraid to face the responsibility of being king. Like Saul—and like me—it's not uncommon to experience fear when stepping into a calling. We often feel unworthy of the task before us. But Saul's hiding wasn't an act of humility—it was an act of fear. Saul feared that the people wouldn't accept him and follow him as their leader. If God calls you to a task, He will equip you for it. Don't let fear keep you from serving where He has placed you. Whether in your home, church, or work, step forward today. Don't hide in the baggage, God is with you.

**Journal:** Where are you tempted to hide when life feels overwhelming? How can you trust God to equip you for what He has called you to do?

**One-sentence prayer:** Heavenly Father, help me to step out in faith, trusting that You will equip me for what You have called me to do.

***Further hope and encouragement: Psalm 139***

# DAY 124
# Who You Are (When No one is Watching)

*Whoever walks in integrity walks securely, but whoever takes crooked paths will be found out.*
*Proverbs 10:9*

As a school principal, I often encourage and remind kids about integrity—doing the right thing simply because it's the right thing to do. One key line I always add is, "Even when no one is watching." For the most part, kids behave well in the classroom or when they're near an adult, but most problems occur on the playground, in the cafeteria, on the school bus, or in the bathrooms. These are places where kids have more freedom without direct adult supervision. Quite honestly, they are some of the biggest headache locations in schools—the places where no one seems to be watching or where it's harder to see because of the crowd. It's as if kids try so hard to behave when they know they're being watched that, when they get a little "freedom," they let their guard down.

So far, I've written about kids at school, but what about us as adults? It's a simple question—do we do the right thing because it's the right thing to do? Even when no one is watching? Like kids at school, we may be trying so hard to behave and follow God's Word, but then, just like them, do we become weary of doing good when no one is looking? Do we blend in with the crowd instead of standing firm? Is it the television show we watch? The website or social media we scroll? The places we go? Proverbs 10:9 tells us, "Whoever walks in integrity walks securely, but whoever takes crooked paths will be found out." A successful life is defined by obedience to God's Word—even when no one is watching. If we're tired and feel like giving up, rest in this truth: God has given us everything we need and will supply the strength to sustain us today and every day. So let me ask you this—who are you, even when, or should I say, especially when no one is watching?

**Journal:** Where in your life do you find it hardest to do the right thing when no one is watching? How can you remain faithful in those moments?

**One-sentence prayers:** Heavenly Father, help me to walk in integrity, choosing what is right even when no one else sees.

*Further hope and encouragement: Proverbs 10*

# DAY 125
# How Long, O Lord?

*How long, O Lord? Will you forget me forever? How long will you hide your face from me? How long must I wrestle with my thoughts and every day have sorrow in my heart? How long will my enemy triumph over me?*
*Psalm 13:1-2*

Waiting is hard, and I struggle to wait. I want things to happen when I want them to happen. Waiting feels like a waste of time. I have things to do, people to see, and goals to reach. But do you know what I've learned over the years? Waiting reveals and exposes the condition of my heart. The season of my life marked by anxiety and depression was painful. During that time, God directed me to Psalm 13, where David cries out to God four times, asking, "How long?" in his distress. That's exactly how I felt in my struggles—How long will this last? God, where are You? Why me? How long, how long, how long?

Like David at the beginning of Psalm 13, I was consumed by my circumstances, looking for a quick remedy to ease my suffering. I longed to simply pray and have the discomfort disappear overnight or with the snap of my fingers. But just a few verses later, David shifts his gaze from himself to God, declaring, "But I trust in Your unfailing love; my heart rejoices in Your salvation. I will sing to the Lord, for He has been good to me" (vv. 5-6). In my pain and suffering, I began to repeat those words daily: "But I trust in Your unfailing love." Like David, my circumstances didn't change, but through God's grace, my focus did—I turned from myself to Him. I didn't need a quick fix, I needed to trust and submit to what God had already written in His Word. Like David, lift your eyes off your circumstances and fix your gaze on God, trusting in His unfailing love today.

**Journal:** What is the "How long?" in your life that you are wrestling with right now? In what ways have you been searching for answers elsewhere instead of trusting in God's Word? How can you shift your focus from your circumstances to His unfailing love today?

**One-sentence prayer:** Heavenly Father, when I struggle with waiting and uncertainty, help me fix my gaze on You and trust in Your unfailing love.

*Further hope and encouragement: Psalm 13*

# DAY 126
# Feel vs. Know

*The Lord himself goes before you and will be with you; he will never*
*leave you nor forsake you. Do not be afraid; do not be discouraged.*
*Deuteronomy 31:8*

It's easy to get lost in how we feel. We can get stuck in our emotions, letting them dictate our perspective. Think about it—what do we often ask others before a big moment, during a struggle, or in the midst of hardship? "How are you feeling?" Processing our thoughts and emotions is important. We are called to pour out our hearts to God (Psalm 62:8). But we can't stay there. The new job, the big meeting, the difficult relationship, the struggles with marriage or parenting—these all bring feelings. However, instead of asking, "How am I feeling?" we must shift our focus to "What do I know?" More importantly, "Who do I know?" and "What has He already said and done?"

When it was Joshua's time to succeed Moses as the leader of Israel, he was likely nervous—maybe even terrified. Moses, at 120 years old, could no longer lead, and before he died, he told Joshua, "Be strong and courageous" (Deuteronomy 31:7). He assured Joshua that the Lord would go before him, be with him, and never leave him: "Do not be afraid; do not be discouraged" (Deuteronomy 31:8). Then, after Moses died, God Himself spoke to Joshua, saying, "Have I not commanded you? Be strong and courageous. Do not be afraid; do not be discouraged, for the Lord your God will be with you wherever you go" (Joshua 1:9). So, what did Joshua feel? We don't know for certain, but like you and me, he probably wrestled with fear and doubt. But what did Joshua know? He knew that God was with him, that He would never leave him, and that He had already gone before him. It's OK to acknowledge your feelings, but don't stay there too long. Instead, fix your eyes on the truth of God's Word and what you already know to be true. Whatever you're facing today, remember this: it's not about how you feel—it's about what you know and Who you know.

**Journal:** What situation in your life is stirring up feelings of fear, doubt, or uncertainty? How can you shift your focus from how you feel to what you know to be true about God? Search God's Word today and rest in that truth.

**One-sentence prayer:** Heavenly Father, help me to stand on the truth of Your Word rather than be consumed by my feelings, knowing that You are always with me.

***Further hope and encouragement: Joshua 1***

## DAY 127

# Connect, Inspire, Empower

*I have set you an example that you should do as I have done for you.*
*John 13:15*

The school district where I serve as a principal has a simple yet powerful three-word mission statement: "Connecting. Inspiring. Empowering." Those three words beautifully reflect how Jesus led His disciples. When Jesus called His first disciples, He said, "Come, follow me" (Matthew 4:19). He had a clear vision and purpose—not just to gather followers, but to transform lives and send them out to continue His work. He communicated, taught, and modeled His mission, always pointing back to His purpose: doing the will of the One who sent Him (John 6:38). Yet, beyond His teaching, Jesus built deep personal connections with His disciples. He knew their strengths, weaknesses, and potential. No matter where we are—at work, church, or home—we are called to do the same. Taking the time to truly know people, to understand their struggles and aspirations, reflects the heart of Christ.

As we think about our homes, workplaces, and communities, how are we connecting, inspiring, and empowering those around us? Do we take the time to truly see people, to listen, and to invest in their lives? Jesus didn't just lead from a distance—He walked alongside His disciples, shared meals with them, and invited them into His life. Are we building relationships in a way that reflects His love? Are we inspiring others through our words and actions, pointing them toward truth and encouragement? And are we empowering those around us, equipping them with the confidence and tools they need to grow? Jesus took ordinary people and entrusted them with an extraordinary mission. That same call extends to us. When we follow His example—by intentionally connecting, inspiring, and empowering others—we don't just make a difference; we help build God's kingdom.

**Journal:** Think about the people in your life—at home, work, or in your community. How can you be more intentional about connecting, inspiring, and empowering them? What is one specific action you can take this week to follow Jesus' example in building relationships?

**One-sentence prayer:** Heavenly Father, help me to follow Jesus' example by connecting with others, inspiring them through my words and actions, and empowering them to step into the purpose You have for them.

***Further hope and encouragement: Ephesians 4***

# DAY 128
# Shine as a Light

*You are the light of the world. A city set on a hill cannot be hidden.*
*Matthew 5:14*

I write and speak often about overflow. But I don't know if I've ever seen it so evident as I did in Berkis, a school director in the Dominican Republic. Since she was a little girl, she dreamed of working with kids. Alongside her mother, she started a small school with just twenty students, walking the streets of her community to invite more. Over time, the need for quality education became undeniable. When she found an abandoned lot—once a garbage dump—she saw not just what it was, but what it could be. She convinced the owners to let her clean it up and transform it into a school. Today, her school serves 317 students, including the children of her original students—a generational impact in motion.

As we met with Berki in a crowded conference room—with no air conditioning and only a single fan hanging from the ceiling—she radiated joy as she spoke about her students. Her greatest passion is not just teaching, but loving each child in a way that reveals the love of Christ. When asked how we could pray for her, she responded through a translator, and of course, it was something other than herself: "Pray for the kids." Berki shared, "My job is to show the love of the Lord through this school." That is exactly what we are called to do—right where we are. Like her, we are meant to shine as a light, taking our vertical relationship with God and spreading it horizontally to those in our sphere of influence. But Berki didn't just want to impact her students—she wanted to create a ripple effect. She understood that by pouring into these children, they would one day pour into others. She is not just leading; she is multiplying. Like a city on a hill, her light isn't meant to shine in isolation—it is meant to spark other lights, igniting a chain reaction of transformation. Her impact will go beyond her school and her time, shaping not only the students she leads today but also the generations they will one day influence. Impact leads to impact. Overflow leads to more overflow. Berki isn't just changing lives—she's changing legacies. Let's do the same.

**Journal:** Who has overflowed into your life, shaping you into who you are today? How can you do the same for others? Write about one way you can intentionally pour into someone else this week.

**One-sentence prayer:** Heavenly Father, help me to be a light, pouring into others as You have poured into me, so that Your love continues to multiply.

***Further hope and encouragement: Matthew 5:14-16***

## DAY 129
# Chasing Acceptance

*Therefore, if anyone is in Christ, the new creation has come:*
*The old has gone, the new is here!*
*2 Corinthians 5:17*

I have a tendency to wake up in the morning, even though I'm exhausted, and say to myself, "All right, here we go, no rest for the weary." It's like I'm gearing up for another day of striving, pushing forward, and trying to prove myself. One morning, I was reading an article when a single line deeply convicted me: "The gospel frees us to work from a position of acceptance versus in pursuit of acceptance." Ouch. I was a tired husband, dad, principal, and coach that morning. I felt like I was on a hamster wheel—chasing the approval of others but never quite reaching it. No matter how hard I tried, I always felt like I needed to do more. It was exhausting.

David, however, understood something I often forget. He knew the Lord was his Shepherd. He knew his Shepherd would lead him to green pastures and still waters (Psalm 23:1-2). But instead of following, I often try to get out in front of God, searching for rest and acceptance on my own terms, searching for rest in the approval and acceptance of others. Yet, rather than peace, I find only more restlessness. Instead of surrendering and trusting that Jesus is more than enough, I anxiously strive to prove myself day after day. But here's the truth: Pursuing acceptance from others will only leave you restless. True rest can only come through Jesus. He calls us to come to Him, to lay down our striving, and to rest in what He has already done. You are not defined by what you do, but by what Jesus has done for you.

**Journal:** Think about a time when you felt like you had to prove your worth to others. How did that striving make you feel? Now, reflect on what it means to already be fully accepted by God. How would your daily life change if you lived from a place of acceptance rather than striving for it?

**One-sentence prayer:** Heavenly Father, help me to stop striving for acceptance and instead rest in the identity You have given me.

*Further hope and encouragement: Psalm 23*

# DAY 130
# What Matters Most

*But seek first the kingdom of God and his righteousness,*
*and all these things will be added to you.*
*Matthew 6:33*

Pause for a moment and ask yourself: What matters most to me? If it helps, take a moment to write a list. Now, look at the top of that list. Is it Jesus? Your relationship with God? Is your family near the top? Your church? Your work? I'm guessing they are. Now, here's the harder and more convicting question: Is the way you're living your life aligning with what you say matters most? Or is there a disconnect between what you claim is most important and how you actually spend your time and energy?

Peter Greer, author and President of Hope International, joined a group in 2015 called "Eulogists." The seven members made a commitment to live in light of what truly matters. Every January, they meet and reflect honestly on whether they are actually living for what they say is most important. This group was inspired by David Brooks' (2015) *New York Times* article, The Road to Character, which contrasts resume virtues—the skills we bring to the marketplace—with eulogy virtues—the qualities people will remember about us when we're gone. The world constantly pushes us to chase resume virtues—career success, achievements, status. We hear messages like Push harder. You got this. Don't let anyone stand in your way. You deserve it. But at the end of our lives, what will really matter? What will people say about us at our funeral? More importantly, what will they say about Jesus because of the way we lived? Let's not get lost in building an earthly resume and forget to invest in what truly lasts. Live today—and every day—in light of what matters most.

**Journal:** If someone gave your eulogy today, what would they say? Would their words reflect the life you want to live? What changes can you make today to align your life with what truly matters?

**One-sentence prayer:** Heavenly Father, help me to seek You first in all things letting my life reflect what truly matters.

***Further hope and encouragement: Colossians 3***

## DAY 131
# Mission Driven

*"What shall I do, then, with Jesus who is called Christ?*
*Pilate asked. They all answered, "Crucify him!"*
*Matthew 27:22*

We hear lines like these so often: "Know your why," "Lead with purpose," "Be mission-driven." But how often do we let fear of an uncomfortable conversation or the pressure to "go with the crowd" keep us silent? Instead of standing firm, we sweep things under the rug and allow them to pass unaddressed. Personally, I have a tendency to avoid confrontation and the tension that comes with it. Others may confront in the wrong way, causing even more harm to relationships and situations. But here's the thing: it's not about feelings. It's about knowing our purpose and mission in life and ensuring that our words and actions align with that purpose. True faithfulness requires courage—the willingness to stand firm even when it's difficult.

Sometimes, the easiest thing to do in the moment is to people-please. When Jesus was facing crucifixion, Pilate knew it was out of envy that the chief priests were handing Him over. Yet, as the chief priests stirred up the crowd, their cries grew louder: "Crucify him!" (Matthew 27:23). Pilate, seeking to satisfy the crowd, gave in and handed Jesus over to be crucified. He knew what was right but chose to do what was popular. He recognized the jealousy of the leaders but prioritized avoiding rebellion. Jesus, on the other hand, remained mission-driven. He declared, "For I have come down from heaven not to do my will but to do the will of Him who sent me" (John 6:38). That is our calling as well—to remain faithful to God's mission, vision, and values, even when it's not the popular thing to do. Be like Jesus. Be mission-driven.

**Journal:** Where in your life are you tempted to prioritize approval over obedience to God's mission? How can you take one step today to stand firm in your faith?

**One-sentence prayer:** Heavenly Father, help me to stand firm in Your mission for my life, even when it's uncomfortable or unpopular.

***Further hope and encouragement: Matthew 27: 11-26***

# DAY 132
# May It Be as You've Said

*"I am the Lord's servant," Mary answered. "May it be to
me as you have said." Then the angel left her.*
*Luke 1:38*

Have you ever had a plan for your day, only to find that God had a different one? What about a plan for your life, job, or career, only to realize that God had something else in store? As Proverbs 16:9 says, "As human beings we plan our course, but the Lord establishes our steps." Many times in my career, I thought I had my future mapped out, only for God to guide me in a different direction. In full transparency, there were moments when I found myself asking, "God, what are You doing? I don't understand." But looking back, I can see that His plans were always better than mine—even when they didn't make sense in the moment.

Imagine how Mary felt when she was unexpectedly visited by the angel Gabriel and told that she was favored by the Lord, would become pregnant, and give birth to a son named Jesus, who would be called the Son of the Most High, and whose kingdom would never end (Luke 1:28-33). Mary asked one question: "How can this be? I'm a virgin" (Luke 1:34). The angel replied with something humans don't hear every day: "The Holy Spirit will come to you, and the power of the Most High will overshadow you" (Luke 1:35). You would think Mary would have been overwhelmed or terrified—I know I would have. But her response was simple and calm, not worried about the interruptions to her own plans: "I am the Lord's servant. May it be to me as you have said" (Luke 1:38). Mary understood her identity as the Lord's servant and surrendered in humble obedience. Her heart was prepared for God's call, and she responded with complete trust. Are our hearts just as prepared? Like Mary, we must be willing to say, "I am the Lord's servant. May it be to me as You have said," no matter where God leads.

**Journal:** Think about a time when God's plan for your life didn't align with your own. How did you respond? Like Mary, what would it look like to fully trust and surrender to His will, even when you don't understand?

**One-sentence prayer:** Heavenly Father, help me to trust Your plan over my own and to respond with a heart of humble obedience, just as Mary did.

***Further hope and encouragement: Luke 1:26-38***

# DAY 133
# Your Kingdom Come

*Your kingdom come, your will be done on earth as it is in heaven.*
*Matthew 6:10*

Jesus taught us to pray these seven words as part of the Lord's Prayer: "Your kingdom come, your will be done" (Matthew 6:10). But when we pause and think about these words, can we truly say them and mean them with all our hearts? Jesus showed us and taught us how to pray and live with an ambassador mentality. Notice that Jesus didn't say, "My kingdom come, my will be done." Instead, His prayer was outward-focused—that His heart would align with God's heart in all that He thought, said, and did. Sadly, if you're anything like me, we get lost in the day-to-day of building our own kingdoms, believing we deserve things with a my, my, my mentality.

So today, join me in quieting our hearts so that our gaze may be fixed only on our Heavenly Father. In all areas of our lives, let's say, "Your kingdom come, your will be done."

Heavenly Father, may Your kingdom come and Your will be done in all that I do, say, and think. May Your kingdom come and Your will be done in every single one of my relationships. May Your kingdom come and Your will be done in the decisions that sit before me today. May Your kingdom come and Your will be done in the steps You have planned for my life. May Your kingdom come and Your will be done in every conversation today. May Your kingdom come and Your will be done when things are going as planned, when they are not going as planned, and when I'm unsure of what's next. May, as Jesus spoke, "Your kingdom come, your will be done, on earth as it is in heaven."

**Journal:** In what areas of your life are you more focused on building your own kingdom rather than seeking God's kingdom? What would it look like today to surrender those areas to Him?

**One-sentence prayer:** Heavenly Father, may Your kingdom come, may Your will be done.

*Further hope and encouragement: Matthew 6:9-13*

# DAY 134
# Purposeful

*For God is not a God of disorder but of peace.*
*1 Corinthians 14:33*

Do you ever feel like you're stuck on the merry-go-round of life? You're spinning round and round, unable to see clearly. Just when it slows down for a moment, you feel disoriented—only for someone to start spinning you again. It's a cycle that makes you feel like you've lost all control. One evening, I found myself completely overbooked after once again saying "yes" too much. I had scheduled or agreed to multiple events, all of which were good things—important meetings, opportunities to connect, and things I cared deeply about. I convinced myself I could make them all work. But I rushed from one thing to the next—barely present in any of them—until I finally collapsed onto the couch at the end of the night, exhausted and frustrated. In trying to be everywhere, I had been nowhere. My schedule was running me instead of the other way around.

That night, I realized that in the midst of my busyness, I had allowed chaos to take over as I moved from one commitment to the next. Before I knew it, I wasn't living a purpose-driven life but a chaos-driven one. And I was tired of it because I knew this wasn't the way God intended me to live. God is a God of peace and order, not chaos. The way we live says something about God—either something true or something false. As 1 Corinthians 14:33 reminds us, "For God is not a God of disorder but of peace." Jesus didn't come to do His own will but the will of the One who sent Him. Everything He did aligned with His Heavenly Father. He was intentional about spending time with God every day and lived in a rhythm of purposeful work. It's time to be more purposeful in what we say yes to—and when we say no. We must step off the merry-go-round, quiet the chaos, and realign our lives with the peace and purpose God intends for us.

**Journal:** Where in your life have you allowed busyness to take over, and how can you be more intentional about living with God's peace and purpose? How can you be more purposeful in what you say yes to and when you say no?

**One-sentence prayer:** Heavenly Father, help me step off the merry-go-round of busyness and align my life with Your peace and purpose.

***Further hope and encouragement: Genesis 1***

DAY 135

# What Do You Need to Give Up?

*Then he said to them all: "If anyone would come after me, he must
deny himself and take up his cross daily and follow me."*
*Luke 9:23*

Today's devotion convicts me deeply. The title itself is staring me in the
face. I know I need to address it, but I often try to avoid reflecting on
it—because, truth be told, I don't like giving things up. If you're like
me, you're busy—too busy. What fills your schedule? What consumes your
mind? How do you spend your free time, even just a few spare moments? As I
flip through my journal, I notice a recurring question: What do I need to give
up? What's holding me back? What's weighing me down from fully following
Jesus? What's adding stress, anxiety, or worry to my life?

A few years ago, Carly and I decided to purchase a used boat off Facebook
Marketplace. We love spending time on the water as a family—water skiing,
tubing, and making great memories. But do you know what my favorite part of
the boating day is? Backing the boat into my grandparents' barn and unhook-
ing it. You see, although we enjoy the time on the water, I'm always nervous
when I'm pulling the boat. I have to drive slower. I worry about every bump
and turn. I get anxious backing it into the water and pulling it out. There's a
constant pull, a heaviness that makes every mile feel longer. But then, when I
unhook that boat in the barn—total relief. Jesus makes it clear in Luke 9:23,
"If anyone would come after me, he must deny himself and take up his cross
daily and follow me." Following Jesus requires daily surrender. It's a willingness to lay down whatever is weighing us down—our distractions, our pride,
our need for control—so we can walk freely in obedience to Him. What are
you holding onto that you need to let go of? Unhook it and follow Jesus.

**Journal:** What's something in your life that feels like a heavy burden right
now? What would it look like to unhook it and trust Jesus instead?

**One-sentence prayer:** Heavenly Father, help me recognize what's weighing me down and give me the courage to unhook it fully into Your hands.

*Further hope and encouragement: Luke 9:18-27*

## DAY 136
# Don't Fight Your Battles Alone

*Carry each other's burdens, and in this way you will fulfill the law of Christ.*
*Galatians 6:2*

"You can't do it all yourself. Quit trying to." Carly has told me those two sentences far more times than I would like to admit. Too often, I find myself putting my head down and working hard, thinking I can push through any challenge on my own. This approach often leads me to points of exhaustion and isolation. Over time, I've realized that sometimes we just need to ask for help. It doesn't even have to be anything serious or life-changing—it could be something as simple as sharing a task or seeking advice. The question is: how can we build habits of walking alongside others and leaning on them when we need support?

We are called to carry each other's burdens (Galatians 6:2). Scripture is full of examples that demonstrate the power of doing life together. Jesus often sent the disciples out two by two (Mark 6:7). David had Jonathan. Ruth had Naomi. Moses had Aaron. Paul frequently traveled with companions like Barnabas, Silas, and Timothy. So, let me ask you this: Who are you surrounding yourself with? Who is your trusted go-to person? Are you creating space in your life to ask for help or to walk alongside others? God places people in our lives for a reason. We need them and they need us. They strengthen, encourage, and protect us during difficult times, just as we are called to do for them. Don't fight your battles alone.

**Journal:** Who in your life has walked alongside you during challenging times? How can you be intentional about asking for help or supporting someone else this week?

**One-sentence prayer:** Heavenly Father, thank you for the people You've placed in my life.

***Further hope and encouragement: Ruth 1***

# DAY 137
# Growing Pains

*Being confident of this, that he who began a good work in*
*you will carry it on to completion until the day of Christ Jesus.*
*Philippians 1:6*

I remember, as a young kid, calling out to my mom from my bed because I couldn't sleep. She would come into my room and ask what was wrong. I told her my legs hurt, and it was an uncomfortable feeling I couldn't fully explain. She gently explained that the discomfort in my legs was growing pains, and it meant I was growing. Of course, as a young boy, I was excited about that—I wanted to grow tall, big, and strong. But even so, I told her I still couldn't sleep when my legs felt that way. Her response was simple yet profound: "Talk to Jesus. When you can't sleep, God wants to spend time with you."

That memory brings me to tears every time I share it. Later in life, during a season of deep sorrow and restlessness, I once again found myself unable to sleep. Much like my childhood experience with growing pains and restless legs, I felt uncomfortable and unsettled. During those long nights, I remembered my mom's words: "You're growing. I know it's uncomfortable right now, but God is growing you for what's to come." Just as Philippians 1:6 reminds us, "being confident of this, that he who began a good work in you will carry it on to completion until the day of Christ Jesus." In those moments of discomfort, I realized that the growth I was experiencing, though difficult, was a part of God's plan to shape me for the future. As my mom reminded me then and I want to remind you now, "Talk to Jesus. God wants to spend time with you." Let me ask you this: How is God growing you in this season? Turn to Him and trust Him. It may not be easy right now, but growth is often uncomfortable. Embrace the growing pains—God is in control.

**Journal:** How have you experienced "growing pains" in your faith, relationships, or personal life? Reflect on how you see God at work in these areas.

**One-sentence prayer:** Heavenly Father, help me to trust You in the seasons of growth, even when it's uncomfortable, knowing that You are shaping me for what's to come.

***Further hope and encouragement: Philippians 1***

## DAY 138

# Lose Yourself

*For whoever wants to save his life will lose it,*
*but whoever loses his life for me will find it.*
Matthew 16:25

I naturally like when things are easy or convenient. I prefer doing things that I know I'll benefit from. I'm the kind of guy who likes to do things when I feel like it. I didn't realize how selfish I naturally was (and still am) until I got married. Taking it a step further, my selfishness was even more apparent when I became a parent. Sometimes I call my kids "little heart shapers" because I know God isn't just using me to point them to Him—He's using them to point me to Him. Through God's grace, He has exposed the selfishness of my heart through marriage and parenting. I wake up wanting what I want, when I want it, desiring for the day to go according to my plans.

Let's look at–and to–Jesus today. It humbles me and brings me to tears to picture Jesus arrested, beaten, and nailed to the cross. Every time I hold the communion cup, I picture His blood dripping into it. As you read in the opening paragraph, I'm a fallen sinner in desperate need of God's grace. I fall short every single day. But through God's grace, we can look to Jesus. There is no better example of a selfless, obedient servant than Jesus. He did not come to do His own will but the will of the One who sent Him. He followed God's will every step of the way—not just when it was easy, convenient, or when He would benefit from it, but even when it was hard, inconvenient, and required sacrifice for a higher purpose. Jesus didn't live His life on earth for Himself; He lived it for His Heavenly Father, the One who sent Him. He lived as an ambassador of God's kingdom. What a powerful and transformational example for us to follow: the Good Shepherd who laid down His life for His sheep.

**Journal:** In what areas of your life are you holding on to selfish desires or personal plans instead of surrendering to God's will? How can you follow Jesus' example of selflessness and obedience this week?

**One-sentence prayer:** Heavenly Father, help me to lose my selfish desires and follow You wholeheartedly.

***Further hope and encouragement: Matthew 16:21-28***

DAY 139

# The Power of a Prayer Notebook

*Therefore encourage one another and build each other up,*
*just as in fact you are doing.*
*1 Thessalonians 5:11*

In my book *Leading with People: A Six Pillar Framework for Fruitful Leadership* (2023), I shared how a principal once encouraged me to keep a little black notebook—and it's a practice that has shaped not just my leadership, but my life. The idea was simple: keep a record of the needs, struggles, and celebrations of the people around you. It doesn't have to be a little black book, of course—any journal or notebook will do. But finding a place to intentionally document these details can be a powerful way to care for others. When we take the time to learn the stories of the people in our lives, we respond with greater compassion and lift them up more purposefully in prayer. As 1 Thessalonians 5:11 reminds us, "Therefore encourage one another and build each other up, just as in fact you are doing."

This notebook can become both a prayer guide and a tool for meaningful connection. By noting specific dates or milestones—whether it's checking in during a hard time or celebrating a moment of joy—we show that we care beyond surface-level interactions. A small follow-up—a card, a text, or a simple check-in—can make a world of difference. Milestones like anniversaries, doctor's appointments, or personal victories offer us moments to affirm that others are seen, known, and valued. Keeping track of these things helps keep our relationships rooted in love and empathy. We aren't called to simply go through the motions of daily life—we're called to genuinely care for one another. A prayer notebook is one small but powerful way to do just that.

**Journal:** Whose stories, needs, or celebrations could you begin writing down and praying over? How might this deepen your relationships and bring encouragement to others?

**One-sentence prayer:** Heavenly Father, help me to live with compassion, remembering and lifting up the needs and joys of those around me.

*Further hope and encouragement: 1 Thessalonians 5*

# DAY 140
# What's Ruling Your Heart?

*My people have committed two sins: They have forsaken me, the spring of living water, and have dug their own cisterns, broken cisterns that cannot hold water.*
*Jeremiah 2:13*

As I write this morning, I feel a deep conviction. We serve an awesome God, don't we? He is good and has blessed me abundantly. But what have I done with His blessings? I've taken them and allowed them to become idols ruling my heart. Whether it's my role as a school leader, husband, father, the books I've written, speaking engagements, or coaching—what started as blessings from God have, at times, become idols. My desire for more can feel insatiable, as though nothing is ever enough. It's not that these things are bad. They're good gifts from God. But when I'm not careful, I start to love the gifts more than the Giver. My heart gets misaligned, and instead of relying on Him, I try to satisfy my thirst on my own—and it never works. Paul Tripp (2014) describes it perfectly, "a desire for a good thing becomes a bad thing when that desire becomes a ruling thing."

How about you? Take a moment to reflect honestly. Have you taken God's blessings and allowed them to rule your heart? Do they consume your thoughts, impact your sleep, influence your words, or drive your actions? Is there a thirst you can't quench? Jeremiah 2 reminds us of Israel's story. God blessed His people abundantly. He led them out of Egypt, through the wilderness, and into a fertile land. But they took their eyes off the Giver and focused on His gifts. God says, "My people have exchanged their glory for worthless idols" (Jeremiah 2:11). He goes on to say, "My people have committed two sins: They have forsaken me, the spring of living water, and have dug their own cisterns, broken cisterns that cannot hold water" (Jeremiah 2:13). The truth is, we can never quench our thirst on our own. Only Jesus, the spring of living water, can satisfy us fully. So, let me ask you today: What's ruling your heart? The gifts from the Giver—or the Giver Himself?

**Journal:** What blessings in your life have you allowed to take a place in your heart that belongs to God? How can you shift your focus back to the Giver rather than the gifts?

**One-sentence prayer:** Heavenly Father, help me to recognize the idols in my heart and turn back to You, the only One who can truly satisfy my soul.

***Further hope and encouragement: Jeremiah 2***

## DAY 141
# God Will Provide

*Find rest, O my soul, in God alone; my hope comes from him. He alone
is my rock and my salvation; he is my fortress, I will not be shaken.*
*Psalm 62:5-6*

While on a trip to the Dominican Republic, our family met an employee named Astia from the Esperanza staff. *Esperanza* means "hope" in Spanish. Astia is the Branch Office Manager of Esperanza in Santo Domingo, working to restore dignity to the people of the Dominican Republic while proclaiming the gospel of Christ through the powerful tool of Christ-centered microfinance. Over lunch one day, someone asked her if she had ever thought about leaving her job for something else. In response, she shared a story. She explained that on the days she feels stressed and exhausted—days when she thinks about giving up or doing something different—God always provides what she needs. Whether through an interaction or a conversation, He gives her the encouragement to keep going.

In those moments, she has learned to rest in God, trusting that He is her rock, her salvation, and her fortress—just as Psalm 62:5-6 reminds us. Because of that, she is not shaken. As you wake up today, maybe you feel like Astia—exhausted, stressed, unsure if you can keep going. Maybe it's your job, parenting, marriage, or the endless, mundane tasks that seem to pile up day after day. Hold onto this truth: when you feel like you have nothing left to give, the Lord will provide. I have those days, too—days I'd rather hide than face what's ahead. But the days you feel like you can't move forward in your own strength are the days God calls you to move forward in His, and that's the perfect place to be. Watch what He does. Look for an interaction, a conversation, a text message, or a phone call today. God will use you—just watch. He will provide.

**Journal:** What is an area of your life where you feel like you have nothing left to give? How can you intentionally rest in God's strength today rather than your own?

**One-sentence prayer:** Heavenly Father, when I feel weak and weary, help me to trust that You will always provide what I need.

*Further hope and encouragement: Psalm 62*

# DAY 142
# No Language Barrier

*But the fruit of the Spirit is love, joy, peace, patience, kindness, goodness,
faithfulness, gentleness, and self-control. Against such things there is no law.*
*Galatians 5:22-23*

As I walked into the classrooms of schools in the Dominican Republic, I wanted so badly to talk with the kids. Unfortunately, I know very little Spanish, and the kids knew very little English. But here's what we could do together—and we loved it: we smiled at one another, we high-fived, we gave fist bumps, and we hugged. There was no language barrier when it came to showing kindness.

One of the fruits of the Spirit is kindness (Galatians 5:22-23). We are called to be kind—not just to people who look like us, talk like us, or treat us well. We are called to be kind to all people, in all places, at all times. Kindness isn't just something we do when we feel like it; it's a reflection of Christ's love in us. Jesus showed us the greatest kindness when He laid down His life for us on the cross, and because of His love, we can extend that same kindness to others. Like those kids in the Dominican Republic, offer a high-five, a fist bump, a hug, or even just a smile to someone today. Kindness doesn't require words—it simply requires a willing heart. Through God's grace, we can be a reflection of His love in every interaction. Because in the end, there's no language barrier when it comes to kindness.

**Journal:** Who has shown you Christ-like kindness in your life? How can you intentionally extend that same kindness to someone today, even if it's in a small way?

**One-sentence prayer:** Heavenly Father, help me to reflect Your love through kindness, showing grace to all people just as You have shown grace to me.

***Further hope and encouragement: 1 Corinthians 13***

## DAY 143
# Hope

*We have this hope as an anchor for the soul, firm and secure.*
*Hebrews 6:19*

We all put our hope in something.
I hope I get that job.
I hope the weather is nice.
I hope my favorite restaurant is open.
I hope my kids are obedient.
I hope my spouse changes their heart.
I hope things get better.
Hope, hope, hope.
Every day, we place our hope in something.

But too often, we put our hope in things of this world—people, circumstances, outcomes, things beyond our control. And when those things fail us, disappointment follows. But real hope—true, unshakable hope—is not found in circumstances. It's not found in success, in relationships, in money, or even in good health.

Hope is only found in grace.

And that grace is Jesus.

Scripture reminds us: We have this hope as an anchor for the soul, firm and secure (Hebrews 6:19). Jesus is the only hope that never fails, the anchor that holds us steady when life's storms rage. He is the hope that carries us when we are weary, the hope that remains when everything else fades. So don't put your hope in the things of this world. People and things will always let you down. Put your hope in Jesus, the One who wore the thorny crown. The One who conquered death. The One who will never leave you nor forsake you. Because when your hope is in Him, you will never be shaken.

**Journal:** What are you placing your hope in today? Are you trusting in things that can fade, or in the unshakable hope of Jesus? Write about one way you can shift your hope to Christ this week.

**One-sentence prayer:** Heavenly Father, be my only hope—steady my heart, anchor my soul, and help me trust in You alone.

***Further hope and encouragement: Hebrews 6:13-20***

## DAY 144
# Love Well

*Husbands, love your wives, just as Christ loved
the church and gave himself up for her.*
*Ephesians 5:25*

As I flipped through my journal recently, I noticed a recurring theme: I often fall short in loving Carly the way she deserves—and the way I'm called to love her. One entry read, "I need to pursue my spouse. I need to love Carly better, listen to her, be present with her, be intentional with her. Too many times I miss the mark." I'll improve for a week or two, but then old habits creep back in. This cycle reveals the reality of my heart and priorities. Still, I've learned a vital truth: when I'm loving Carly well, everything else in life feels more grounded. And when my relationship with Carly is off, everything else feels off, too. A mentor and friend of mine, now passed, would often ask me, "Zac, how well are you loving your wife?" His advice always stayed with me: "The answer should always be, 'Not as well as I should.'" It's a humbling reminder of the continuous effort love requires.

I don't know your age, gender, or relationship status. But if you're married, are you loving your spouse well? If you're engaged, are you laying the foundation to love well in your marriage? If you're not in a relationship, how are you loving the people around you—your family, your friends, your community? Far too often, we pour ourselves into work, school, or personal goals and forget the people closest to us. During my journey to earn a principal certification and doctorate degree, no course ever emphasized the importance of caring well for my spouse or those closest to me. Yet Scripture does. Paul's call in Ephesians 5:25 to love sacrificially mirrors Christ's ultimate act of love. It's a high standard—and today's verse is a convicting one. I fall short daily. But praise God for His grace and mercy. Love is foundational to life. It's not something we master once—it's something we practice, imperfectly but persistently, every single day. Start where you are. Love well, today.

**Journal:** Think about your closest relationships. How well are you loving them? What's one way you can be more intentional this week?

**One-sentence prayer:** Heavenly Father, help me love those closest to me well today.

*Further hope and encouragement: Ephesians 5:25-28,*
*1 Corinthians 13:4-8*

DAY 145

# Peace of Mind

*You will keep in perfect peace him whose mind is*
*steadfast, because he trusts in you.*
*Isaiah 26:3*

D o you have peace of mind today? Or is your peace drowned out by the worries of this world? Did you sleep well last night, or did you lie awake fearing the future? We often try to find peace by controlling our circumstances—securing finances, managing relationships, or planning every detail of our lives. But true peace isn't found in control. True peace is found in surrender. I've written before about Alisabeth and her sewing business in the Dominican Republic, made possible through microfinance loans. When we visited her, she told our group, "I have peace of mind every day because I know that every loan is prayed over." Alisabeth doesn't have much from a material standpoint, yet she has something far greater—faith. Faith that even when she can't see it, God is working. Faith that He will provide, time and time again.

Why? Because she trusts in the power of prayer. She believes in what God has done, what He is doing, and what He will do. Alisabeth controls what she can and surrenders everything else to Him. And what can she truly control? Nothing. Instead, she chooses to trust in God, resting in the promise that He will keep in perfect peace those whose minds are steadfast because they trust in Him (Isaiah 26:3). The world tells us that peace comes from security, comfort, and success. But God's peace is different. His peace isn't based on our circumstances—it surpasses them. We often make life more complicated than it has to be. We hold on to things we were never meant to carry. We worry about what we don't need to worry about. But through God's grace, we can follow Alisabeth's example—resting in prayer and finding peace in the One who holds all things together.

**Journal:** What worries are keeping you from experiencing God's perfect peace? Spend a few moments in prayer, surrendering those burdens to Him, and ask for a steadfast heart that trusts in His plans.

**One-sentence prayer:** Heavenly Father, help me to release my worries and trust in You, knowing that true peace is only found in Your presence.

**Further hope and encouragement: Matthew 6:25-34**

# DAY 146
# Try New Things

*Forget the former things; do not dwell on the past. See I am doing*
*a new thing! Now it springs up; do you not perceive it? I am*
*making a way in the desert and streams in the wasteland.*
*Isaiah 43:18-20*

I was traveling with the Hoober family in another country when I heard the dad share the following line to his three young kids: "The Hoobers try new things." As a father of a young family, and someone who likes the familiar myself, I loved that quote. I asked him about it, and he explained that they encourage their kids to step out of their comfort zone, to leave the familiar behind, and try new things. Whether it's food, an activity, or something else, they encourage their kids to give it a try at least once, and they model this behavior themselves. He joked that they may have to alter that motto as the kids get older, explaining that they don't need to try everything in this world.

Here's the thing: some of their favorite things would have never been tried if they didn't give it a chance. When I was eight years old, my parents forced me to give basketball a try. I cried the whole way there, but it eventually became my favorite sport and had a tremendous impact on my life. At Disney World, I cried when my parents made me try the Tower of Terror, but it became my favorite ride. Those are only small examples, but I know I don't like to try new things—I love the familiar. But sometimes, just like God spoke to the Israelites in Isaiah 43:18-19, we need to forget the old ways and embrace the new things He has planned for us. If we always stay in what's familiar, we miss the growth and experiences that can only come by stepping into the unknown. God is always doing a new thing in our lives, and we're invited to trust Him in the process. Are you stuck in the familiar? Listen to the words of the Hoobers and "try new things."

**Journal:** What is something new God is calling you to try or step into? How might stepping out of your comfort zone lead to growth in your life?

**One-sentence prayer:** Heavenly Father, help me to embrace the new things You are doing in my life and trust that You have good plans for me beyond what's familiar.

***Further hope and encouragement: Isaiah 43***

## DAY 147
# The Journey

*Not only so, but we also rejoice in our sufferings, because we know that suffering produces perseverance; perseverance, character; and character, hope.*
*Romans 5:3-4*

As we landed in Newark, New Jersey, late one night, our family knew we still had a two-and-a-half-hour drive ahead of us to reach the comfort of home. Isaac, our youngest at the time, seven years old, said what we were all thinking: "I wish I could just snap my fingers, and we would be home." We often hear the question, "If you could have one superpower, what would it be?" Many people, like my son (and probably most of us), wish for teleportation to get to our destination faster. But here's the thing about life: we need the journey. The journey is where God softens and shapes our hearts. The journey is where God grows us to be more like Jesus. It's where we struggle—whether it's through a health battle, a difficult relationship, challenges at work, or struggles at home. The journey is where we come to the end of ourselves. It's where we realize how much we need others along the way. The journey is where we recognize how little strength we have on our own.

Much like the way a sports team doesn't just snap their fingers to reach the championship, we can't skip the hard work and the growth that comes from the journey. A team doesn't make it to the top without countless hours of practice, wins, losses, preparation, teamwork, sweat, injuries, smiles, and tears. It's all part of the process—just as life's journey is. Like my son, we often want to skip ahead to the end, to a place of comfort and rest. But just as Romans 5:3-4 tells us, "suffering produces perseverance; perseverance, character; and character, hope," it's the challenges along the way that refine us and prepare us for what lies ahead. The journey, though hard, is where we find Jesus, look to Jesus, and cling to Jesus. So, trust God in your journey today. Let go of the need for shortcuts and embrace the process, knowing that He's shaping you every step of the way.

**Journal:** Where do you see God at work in your journey right now? How can you trust Him in the process rather than just waiting for the destination?

**One-sentence prayer:** Heavenly Father, help me to trust You in the journey, knowing that You are working in me every step of the way.

*Further hope and encouragement: Romans 5:1-11*

# DAY 148
# Keep Going

*Remember how the Lord your God led you all the way in the*
*wilderness these forty years, to humble and test you in order to know*
*what was in your heart, whether or not you would keep his commands.*
*Deuteronomy 8:2*

It had been a long day in the Dominican Republic, filled with field visits. As evening approached, we were finally heading back for dinner and rest. But as we settled into our seats, Jeff Rutt, founder of Hope International, asked, "Are we going to visit any villages farther outside the city?" Our trip host hesitated. "It would add a lot of time," she said. "It's out of the way, and we won't get back until very late." It would have been easy to call it a day, but Jeff responded with words that stuck with me: "Let's keep going—we will never be closer." Exhausted, we pushed forward for one more stop.

The Israelites knew exhaustion, too. For forty years, they wandered in the wilderness, often wondering if they would ever reach the Promised Land. Some wanted to turn back to Egypt because it felt easier. But God was leading them, shaping them, and teaching them to trust Him. Their journey had a purpose—even when it felt long and difficult. Maybe you're in a season where giving up seems tempting. You've worked hard, but the finish line still feels far away. Keep going. Deuteronomy 8:2 reminds us that God is with us in the wilderness, humbling us, testing us, and revealing what's in our hearts. The struggles you face today are preparing you for something greater. That night in the Dominican Republic, pressing on through exhaustion was worth it. Our last stop turned out to be one of our favorites—we even played baseball with kids in the streets. How cool is that? What if we had turned back? What if we had settled for comfort instead of pressing on? We would have missed out on something incredible. The same is true for you. So today, wherever you are in your journey—don't turn back. Keep going. You will never be closer.

**Journal:** What is something in your life that you've been tempted to give up on because it feels too hard? How might God be using this challenge to strengthen your faith and perseverance?

**One-sentence prayer:** Heavenly Father, when I feel tired and ready to turn back, give me the strength to keep going.

***Further hope and encouragement: Deuteronomy 8:2-4***

# DAY 149
# The Mirror

*Anyone who listens to the word but does not do what it says is like someone who looks at his face in a mirror and, after looking at himself, goes away and immediately forgets what he looks like.*
James 1:23-24

D o you remember the movie *Cool Runnings*? It's an uplifting story about Jamaican sprinters who failed to qualify for the Olympics in their sport but formed a bobsled team to get there. One of the teammates, Jr., struggles with confidence. In a powerful scene, his teammate Yul stands him in front of a mirror and says, "Now tell me what you see." At first, Jr. only sees his flaws, but Yul reminds him of his worth, calling out the strength and potential he doesn't recognize in himself. We do the same thing. When we look at a group picture, we judge its quality based on how we look. When we pass by a mirror, our eyes immediately find our flaws. We are quick to focus on what's wrong, what's lacking, what isn't enough. But that's not what God sees. Far too often, we look into the wrong mirrors. Instead of being shaped by the world's distorted reflections, we need to look into the only mirror that truly matters—the pure, unchanging Word of God.

The Bible is filled with truth, and we must be in it daily to combat the lies that tell us we don't measure up. James 1:23-25 says, "Anyone who listens to the word but does not do what it says is like someone who looks at his face in a mirror and, after looking at himself, goes away and immediately forgets what he looks like. But the man who looks intently into the perfect law that gives freedom, and continues to do this—not forgetting what he has heard, but doing it—he will be blessed in what he does." The world's mirrors tell us we're not good enough, attractive enough, or successful enough. They cause us to compare, to covet, and to live in anxiousness and fear. But when we look into the mirror of God's Word, we see the truth: we are fully loved, accepted, and known. Because of what Jesus did on the cross, we can rest in our identity as children of God. What mirror are you looking in today?

**Journal:** What "mirror" have you been looking into lately? How has it shaped your thoughts about yourself? Take time to reflect on what God's Word says about your true identity.

**One-sentence prayer:** Heavenly Father, help me to see myself through Your eyes and to find my worth in Your truth.

***Further hope and encouragement: James 1:19-27***

# DAY 150
# Nathan

*The Lord sent Nathan to David. When he came to him, he said,*
*"There were two men in a certain town, one rich and the other poor."*
*2 Samuel 12:1*

According to Paul Tripp (2014), "Self-examination is a community project." Simply put, we don't just need people in our lives—we need people who will walk beside us, speaking truth into our lives. We need to surround ourselves with those who will lift us up with encouragement when we need it and have uncomfortable conversations with us when they see us veering off the path we should be on. We may think we know ourselves well, but when we isolate ourselves—whether intentionally or not—we can become blind to our struggles and shortcomings. It's also easy to surround ourselves with "yes-men" or "yes-women" who only tell us what we want to hear.

After King David committed adultery with Bathsheba and orchestrated the murder of Uriah, Nathan confronted him with wisdom and courage, using a parable to open David's eyes to his wrongdoing (2 Samuel 12). When David heard the parable, he "burned with anger" against the man in the story for his actions (v. 5). Then Nathan said to David, "You are the man!" (v. 7). Here's the thing: Nathan wasn't just there for that moment of confrontation. He had been by David's side throughout his journey to becoming King of Israel—always loyal, always providing wise counsel. So, who is the Nathan in your life? And are you a Nathan to someone else? Surround yourself with people who will hold you accountable, speak truth in love, provide spiritual guidance, prevent isolation, restore and grow you, and live with integrity. Every David needs a Nathan—to succeed according to God's definition of success: obedience to Him with humility, wisdom, and a heart that seeks after His own.

**Journal:** Who are the "Nathans" in your life—those who speak truth to you in love and hold you accountable? How can you be a Nathan to someone else?

**One-sentence prayer:** Heavenly Father, surround me with people who will speak truth into my life, and help me to be a faithful friend who does the same with wisdom, courage, and love.

***Further hope and encouragement: 2 Samuel 12***

# DAY 151
# Lead with Grace

*And God is able to make all grace abound to you, so in all things at all times,*
*having all that you need you will abound in every good work.*
*2 Corinthians 9:8*

We are all leaders. Maybe you don't see yourself as a leader, but you are. We all have influence on the people around us—our families, friends, coworkers, and communities. Whether we recognize it or not, the way we live, speak, and act impacts others. That's why we must lead with grace. Every role we serve in is not a result of personal strength or talent. It's not based on anything we've done. Every role is entirely rooted in God's grace, and that grace should shape how we live.

All of our work belongs to God.

The ability to lead is a gift of God's grace.

The call to lead is a gift of God's grace.

Every opportunity to lead is a gift of God's grace.

Being equipped to do God's work is a gift of God's grace.

Faithful obedience in leadership is a gift of God's grace.

God supplies everything we need—wisdom, patience, strength, resources—whatever it may be. He gives us what we need, when we need it. But too often, we try to live from a place of self-sufficiency, forgetting that it is God who equips and enables us for every challenge and opportunity. Grace-filled leadership—and grace-filled living—begins with humility, recognizing that without God's grace, we have nothing to offer. Only when we acknowledge that everything flows from Him can we truly abound in every good work. We no longer have to strive in our own strength. Instead, we can rest in God's provision and faithfully carry out His will. Take a deep breath. Walk in His grace. Lead with His grace today.

**Journal:** Where in your life do you struggle to see yourself as a leader? How can you lean on God's grace rather than your own strength in those areas?

**One-sentence prayer:** Heavenly Father, help me to lead and live from a place of Your grace, relying not on my own strength but on Your endless supply.

***Further hope and encouragement: 2 Corinthians 9:6-15***

# What's Your Prison?

*"Naked I came from my mother's womb, and naked I will depart. The Lord gave and the Lord has taken away; may the name of the Lord be praised."*
*Job 1:21*

"I needed prison." Those words hit me hard as I spoke with an inmate at San Quentin Rehabilitation Center. This man had already been incarcerated for many years and wouldn't be eligible for parole for another twelve. He was a father of two girls and had once been married, but his wife divorced him while he was behind bars. He explained that he had been on a path of destruction with no end in sight. Getting arrested, he said, was both the best and worst thing that ever happened to him. "It brought me to Jesus," he shared, speaking from a place of deep calm and peace. "Without prison, I wouldn't know Jesus at all." I teared up as I listened. So much pain. So much brokenness. So much hurt. But for this man, it was what he needed. Much like Job, who had lost everything and still declared, "May the name of the Lord be praised," this man had lost his freedom, his family, and the life he once knew. Yet he now stood in that loss with a peace that only comes from Jesus—praising God for his circumstances.

So, what about us? What about you? Much like this man needed prison to bring him to Jesus, what is it that you need? Or what is it that you needed? What has drawn—or is drawing—you closer to Jesus? As I reflect on my own life, I can fill in the blank with: "I needed anxiety." Or "I needed depression." These aren't things we typically say we need, but God knows exactly what it takes to bring us back to Him. Scripture reminds us in Job 1:21, "The Lord gave and the Lord has taken away; may the name of the Lord be praised." God gives, and God takes away—not out of cruelty, but out of love. He's always working for our greatest good and His ultimate glory, even when the road is painful. Take a moment today and reflect: how would you fill in the blank? "I needed _____." Maybe yours isn't in the past tense. Maybe something is weighing on you right now, and your line would look more like: "I need _____." What's your prison? What is it you need right now that you need to draw you closer to Jesus?

**Journal:** What difficulty in your life has God used—or is using—to draw you closer to Him? How have you seen His hand at work, even in the loss or pain?

**One-sentence prayer:** Heavenly Father, help me trust that what You give and take is always for my good and Your glory.

***Further hope and encouragement: Job 1, Psalm 34:18***

## DAY 153
# Getting in the Way

*Love the Lord your God with all your heart and with all your*
*soul and with all your mind and with all your strength.*
*Mark 12:30*

You've probably heard it many times: we are called to love God and love people. Notice the order—love for God comes first, and love for others comes second. Far too often, I fall short in this area. I enjoy my quiet morning time—the peace of my coffee as I read God's Word, pray, and write. But then something happens. Carly wakes up. My kids wake up—often way earlier than I think they should. Sometimes I even think, *God, I woke up early to spend time with You. Why are my kids up already?* Then, I go to work, surrounded by people, and before I know it, whether at home or at work, I say or do something I regret. Sometimes, this happens while my Bible is still open! Then it hits me—the very thing I read and prayed about, I had the opportunity to live out, and I fell short. Worshiping God isn't just a morning routine—it's an every-moment-of-every-day thing.

You see, It's often me who gets in my own way, in the way of others, and even in the way of Almighty God. Jesus said the greatest command is: "Love the Lord your God with all your heart, soul, mind, and strength" (Mark 12:30). He continued, "The second is this: 'Love your neighbor as yourself.' There is no commandment greater than these" (v.31). The problem? I like to make myself the center of my universe—my wants, my needs, my plans. When I do, my heart is exposed, and I fail to love and lead others well. Only when we truly love God first can His love overflow into the lives of those around us. When our hearts are set on Him, we reflect His love, joy, peace, patience, kindness, goodness, faithfulness, gentleness, and self-control (Galatians 5:22-23). Give your heart to God in worship today, and watch your cup overflow. Don't let yourself get in the way.

**Journal:** Are you truly putting God first? Reflect on your relationships and interactions—what is overflowing from your heart to others?

**One-sentence prayer:** Heavenly Father, help me keep You first so that my heart overflows with Your love and grace toward others

***Further hope and encouragement: Psalm 63***

# DAY 154
# Wash Feet

*So he got up from the meal, took off his outer clothing, and wrapped a towel around his waist. After that, he poured water into a basin and began to wash his disciples' feet, drying them with the towel that was wrapped around him.*

*John 13:4-5*

The time had come for Jesus "to leave this world and go to the Father" (John 13:1). Pause and think for a moment: What would you do if you knew that tomorrow you would be killed? Many people would focus on completing a bucket list—checking off experiences before they die. But what did Jesus do? He got down on his knees and washed the disciples' feet. Not only that, but he also washed the feet of the one he knew would betray him. Jesus' entire life was marked by humility. He didn't just speak about humility—he lived it out through His actions. Many kings and rulers are untouchable, but Jesus? He knelt and touched the feet of those He served.

What a picture of sacrificial, selfless, humble living. Foot washing was a task reserved for servants, yet Jesus took on this lowly role, setting an example for how we are called to live. Jesus said, "Now that I, your Lord and Teacher, have washed your feet, you also should wash one another's feet. I have set you an example that you should do as I have done for you" (John 13:14–15). Nothing was beneath Jesus. He never used His position for personal gain but chose instead to humbly serve those around Him. Remember, Jesus didn't come to do His own will—he came to do the will of the One who sent him. He deserved the highest place, yet he took on the lowest place for you and me, ultimately laying down his life on the cross. Follow Jesus' example today—wash feet by humbly serving and loving others, even those who may seem unlovable.

**Journal:** Who in your life needs to experience the love of Christ through your humble service? Maybe it's someone you've been struggling with recently. How can you intentionally serve them today?

**One-sentence prayer:** Heavenly Father, help me follow Your example of humility by serving others with a loving and willing heart today.

*Further hope and encouragement: John 13*

## DAY 155

# Live By Faith

*For we live by faith, not by sight.*
*2 Corinthians 5:7*

One morning, as I was driving to work, a dense fog covered my line of sight. It was pitch dark, and I could barely see what was right in front of me. I tried turning on my high beams to see farther ahead, but as we all know, that only made things worse. Thankfully, I had driven this route for years—I knew the curves, turns, and what to watch out for along the way. Though the fog slowed me down, before I knew it, I arrived at school safe and sound, reaching my destination. When I finally saw the school, I took a deep breath and said, "Ah, there it is." Suddenly, things became clear.

We are called to live by faith, not by sight (2 Corinthians 5:7). Much like driving in the fog, sometimes we can only see what's right in front of us. We long to see further ahead, and when we try to take control, we often make things worse—just like high beams in thick fog. Some days or seasons of life are clearer than others, but Charles Spurgeon (n.d) wisely reminds us, "Walk by faith, not by sight, or feelings." You may not know what tomorrow holds, or even what's coming your way today, but you don't have to. Take life moment by moment, day by day, trusting that God is leading the way. He knows the path, He goes before you, and He will guide you through. One day, just as I looked up and realized I had arrived at my destination, you will look back and see how God used every moment to shape and prepare you for eternity. Trust Him in the "fog" today—live by faith, not by sight.

**Journal:** Where in your life do you need to trust God in the "fog" instead of relying on what you can see?

**One-sentence prayer:** Heavenly Father, help me trust You even when I can't see the road ahead.

***Further hope and encouragement: Hebrews 11***

## DAY 156
# What Are You Following Today?

*The Lord is my shepherd, I shall not be in want.*
*Psalm 23:1*

You will follow something or someone today.
Our hearts wake up ready to follow.
Is it your phone? The number of likes on a social media post?
Are you following money? Fame? Self-recognition?
Have you unknowingly turned something good into an idol?
Are you following your heart?
Do you follow people—
Celebrities, athletes, influencers?
Are you chasing acceptance? Trying to be known?
Peering into the lives of others,
Wishing their life was yours?
Do you follow rest? Comfort and ease?
Are you clinging to what's familiar?
Are you chasing the things of this world?
All you want is for your kids to listen to you,
For things to go your way—just once.
For your spouse to understand you.
For your job to feel fulfilling.
For contentment to come easily.
Are you exhausted? Tired? With nothing left to give?
Follow the Good Shepherd today.
He has all that you need.
He will quiet your heart.
He will give you rest.
He will guide you,
When you don't know where to go.
You have nothing to fear,
For He is with you.
His rod and His staff will comfort you.
There is only One worth following.
Follow Jesus today.

**Journal:** What are you most tempted to follow in your daily life? How would your heart and mind change if you fully followed Jesus instead?

**One-sentence prayer:** Heavenly Father, help me to follow You above all else.

*Further hope and encouragement: Psalm 23*

## DAY 157
# Do Not Love the World

*For everything in the world—the cravings of sinful man, the lust of his eyes and the boasting of what he has and does—comes not from the Father but from the world.*
*1 John 2:16*

It was Thanksgiving weekend, and I was running an errand alone. I had never felt emptier than I did during that fifteen-minute drive. Even my gas light was on—an ironic symbol of how I felt inside. The strange thing was that, on paper, I should have been full. I was thirty-eight years old, and in the past few years, I had accomplished so much. I earned my doctorate at 34, published my first book at 36, my second at 37, and now, my third had just been released while I was already writing my fourth. I was speaking across the country, my books were selling, my role as a principal was going well, and my name was growing (notice I said *my* name). By all worldly measures, I was thriving. And yet, there I sat—empty, weary, and tired.

Here's the problem: I had taken the good gifts God had given me and turned them into idols. The more success I tasted, the more I wanted. My focus subtly shifted from advancing His kingdom to advancing my own. I was anxiously awaiting the next achievement, thinking just one more milestone would bring lasting fulfillment. Without realizing it, I had started to love the world. But as 1 John 2:16 warns, "For everything in the world—the cravings of sinful man, the lust of his eyes, and the boasting of what he has and does—comes not from the Father but from the world." I was searching horizontally, believing worldly success could offer security and peace, when the only true peace comes from looking up. I had placed my hope in creation instead of the Creator—the only One who truly satisfies. Maybe you've been there too, chasing the next promotion, the next accomplishment, the next approval, or the next stage of life, believing it will finally fill you. "The world and its desires pass away, but the man who does the will of God lives forever" (1 John 2:17). Let's spend less time striving in the world today and more time resting in the Word.

**Journal:** What are the "good things" in your life that may be subtly pulling your focus away from God? How can you realign your heart to seek fulfillment in Him rather than in success, approval, or achievement?

**One-sentence prayer:** Heavenly Father, You're all I want, You're all I need.

*Further hope and encouragement: 1 John 2:15-17, Ecclesiastes 1*

# DAY 158
# Lay It Down

*The Lord replied, 'My Presence will go with you, and I will give you rest.*
*Exodus 33:14*

Quit trying to carry the weight of the world on your shoulders—you don't have to. Paul Tripp (2014) notes, "You can take life off your shoulders because God has placed it on His." Name every weight that is weighing you down today. As you slow your breath and lower your shoulders, imagine yourself giving each breath to God—each weight to God. Why? Because of Jesus—His birth, life, death, and resurrection—you need not carry the weight of the world. Jesus already has.

Over and over, God's Word tells us to rest in Him when we are tired, thirsty, and weak. "My presence will go with you, and I will give you rest" (Exodus 33:14). In education, we often talk about taking bricks out of a child's backpack. Kids carry so much weight that they can't even focus on learning. God doesn't promise that we won't face burdens of this life, but He does promise that we won't carry them alone. His presence is not distant—it is near, active, and constant. When we surrender our struggles to Him, we exchange our exhaustion for His peace, our striving for His strength. What are the bricks pulling on your shoulders that you're still trying to hold up? Let them go today. Rest in Jesus.

**Journal:** Take a moment to reflect on the burdens you're carrying today—whether it's work, personal struggles, or the weight of others' needs. What are the "bricks" you're holding onto that God is calling you to let go of? Write them down and take a few moments to pray and surrender them to God.

**One-sentence prayer:** Heavenly Father, help me lay down the weight I'm carrying and trust You to carry it for me.

***Further hope and encouragement: Exodus 33***

# DAY 159
# Fellowship with God

*We proclaim to you what we have seen and heard, so that*
*you also may have fellowship with us. And our fellowship*
*is with the Father and with his Son, Jesus Christ.*
1 John 1:3

You have no idea what's coming your way today. You may have a to-do list of tasks you plan to accomplish and a few items on your calendar, but ultimately, you never know how your day will play out. I'm sure you remember the famous *Forrest Gump (1994)* line: "Life is like a box of chocolates. You never know what you're gonna get." First, I love chocolate. And I love a box of chocolates. But no matter how much I study and plan to pick the perfect piece—oh, who am I kidding, pieces—I always end up grabbing the coconut-filled one instead of the peanut butter. And yet, listen closely: I still eat the coconut-filled chocolate—unlike a child who might take a bite and put it back in the box. I also eat the five others I pick before finally finding the peanut butter one I planned on eating.

No matter your role, you can plan your day, but you never truly know how it will unfold. Maybe you wake up expecting a smooth morning, but then your child spills their breakfast, and now you're running late. Maybe you walk into work ready to tackle your agenda, but instead, an urgent situation demands your attention. Or perhaps you anticipate a normal evening with your spouse, only for an unexpected conversation to change everything. *Forrest Gump* was partially right—we don't know exactly what each day holds—we may expect a peanut butter day but end up with coconut or caramel instead. But here's the truth: when our focus is on our Heavenly Father, we do know what we're going to get. No matter how unpredictable or challenging your day may seem, rest in this: God is sovereign over all things. He is in and above everything that comes your way. Put your trust in Him; He will provide everything you need. You're not simply living *for* God today—you're living *with* Him, and He has everything you need. If you are a child of God, you are in fellowship with Him because of Jesus, who lived, died, and rose again for you and me. Let's live and lead in fellowship with God today.

**Journal:** Think about a time when your day didn't go as planned. How did you respond in the moment? Looking back, where do you see God's presence in that situation?

**One-sentence prayer:** Heavenly Father, help me to trust You in every moment today, knowing that You are with me and will provide everything I need.

*Further hope and encouragement: 1 John 1*

## DAY 160
# Time

*He has made everything beautiful in its time. He has also set eternity in the hearts of men; yet they cannot fathom what God has done from beginning to end.*
*Ecclesiastes 3:11*

Do you know what I'm thankful for today? I'm thankful that God is making me more like Jesus every day and not the other way around. I'm too easily satisfied. I like things to happen quickly—sometimes even walking away before a task is fully finished, telling myself, "That's good enough." I get easily distracted...squirrel! My attention span seems to shrink by the day. I grow impatient and irritated when things take too long, often rushing something that is meant to take time. Even something as simple as standing at the microwave feels like a challenge. More often than not, I take my food out with a few seconds left on the timer. Don't worry—I clear the timer. I know some of you out there leave those few seconds for the next person!

Thankfully, everything I just described is me—not our Heavenly Father. He is not easily satisfied. He never stops working until His work is not just finished, but perfected. God doesn't get distracted or grow weary. He isn't impatient or irritated when things don't happen quickly, and He never rushes just to move on to the next task. Psalm 90 gives us a beautiful perspective on God's timing: "Before the mountains were born or you brought forth the earth and the world, from everlasting to everlasting you are God" (v.2). "For a thousand years in your sight are like a day that has just gone by, or like a watch in the night" (v.4). "Teach us to number our days aright, that we may gain a heart of wisdom" (v.10). Unlike me—impatient, distracted, and always in a hurry—God is steady, intentional, and perfectly on time. And that means we can trust that His work in us is unfolding exactly as it should—without a second wasted—for our greatest good and His glory.

**Journal:** Where in your life do you struggle with impatience? How can you trust God's timing in that area?

**One-sentence prayer:** Heavenly Father, help me to trust Your perfect timing and to be patient as You work in my life.

*Further hope and encouragement: Ecclesiastes 3:1-11, Psalm 90*

# DAY 161
# It's Not About You

*For from him and through him and to him are all things.*
*To him be the glory forever! Amen.*
Romans 11:36

I've had to repeat those four words to myself over and over: It's not about you. In fact, I've added a fifth word at the beginning—"Zac, it's not about you." As parents of three kids, Carly and I have lost count of how many times we've had to remind our children of this truth when getting ready to leave for an event. Whether we're dressing them, loading up the car, or heading out the door, there have been plenty of moments when they've complained: Why do we have to go? Each time, we patiently (and sometimes not so patiently) explain that we're going because we care about someone else. Whether it's a gathering, a visit, an event, a funeral, or a birthday party, the focus isn't on us—it's about the people we're going to support. Whether we feel like it or not, it's not about us.

I'm going to say this directly: today is not about you. Yesterday wasn't about you, and tomorrow won't be about you. I say that bluntly because I'm writing this to myself. Those moments with my kids are convicting because God uses them to remind me that I struggle with the same tendencies. Far too often I wake up thinking about me. I lose sight of the fact that life is not about me—my wants, my needs, my desires. No matter our role, we must wake up each day with an "It's not about me" mentality. First, by pursuing God and growing in awe of Him. Second, by allowing Him to shape our hearts to reflect His desires—being His hands and feet in the lives of others. Everything we do should point back to God: "For from him and through him and to him are all things" (Romans 11:36). I'm grateful today is not about me and I'm grateful today is not about you. To God be the glory.

**Journal:** Think about a recent situation where you made something about yourself that wasn't meant to be. How would an "It's not about me" mentality have changed your attitude or response? How can you shift your focus toward God and others today?

**One-sentence prayer:** Heavenly Father, help me to live each day with the humility to remember that life is not about me, but about glorifying You and serving others.

***Further hope and encouragement: Romans 11:33-36***

# DAY 162
# Rich in Love

*The Lord is gracious and compassionate, slow to anger and rich in love.*
*Psalm 145:8*

I learn many life and leadership lessons from Carly, and the one I'm sharing today is a difficult, yet beautiful, one. It was around 6:30 in the morning, and my almost thirteen-year-old daughter was getting ready for school. As I came upstairs after working out, I saw Carly helping our daughter find clothes in a pile of clean laundry. A few moments later, I passed her in the kitchen with tears in her eyes. I immediately went into "rescue mode" and asked what had happened. She walked toward the laundry room, holding up her hand as if to say, "I just need a minute." I then heard her quietly crying in the corner of the laundry room. It wasn't long before I saw her come out, graciously, compassionately, and even cheerfully, continuing to help our daughter.

What a beautiful picture of our Heavenly Father. It was such a representation of the grace and mercy we are given by God every day through His son, Jesus. A little while later, Carly said to me, "It's just hard sometimes." That's exactly right—life is "just hard sometimes," but how do we respond in those hard moments? Do we respond in our human nature to a difficulty at home or at work with impatience or anger? Or do we pause, step away, and respond with grace and compassion because of the grace and compassion we've been given? I will forever remember that scene with Carly. I know she was hurting, frustrated, and it was hard, but in the challenge, Carly showed up and kept loving our daughter, reflecting the love our Father shows us. Today may be hard. Maybe yesterday was hard, or something difficult is coming your way tomorrow. Step away, take a breath, even cry if you need to—then show up, continuing to live and lead cheerfully, rich in love, because of the love we've been given.

**Journal:** Think of a time when, like Carly, you faced a difficult moment. How did you respond? How can you show grace and compassion in those moments, reflecting God's rich love?

**One-sentence prayer:** Heavenly Father, help me to show up in each moment with grace and compassion, reflecting Your rich love to others, especially when it's hard.

***Further hope and encouragement: Genesis 45:4-15, Psalm 145***

## DAY 163

# Go In the Strength That You Have

*The Lord turned to him and said, "Go in the strength you have and save Israel out of Midian's hand. Am I not sending you?"*
*Judges 6:14*

I remember the day I received the phone call offering me the job. After four years as an assistant principal, I was about to step into the role of principal in a new district. Excitement quickly faded and was replaced with self-doubt. Imposter syndrome crept in, and I couldn't shake the thought: What if I can't do this? As an assistant principal, I had always felt "safe," as if I had a safety net to fall back on. Now, the weight of responsibility felt overwhelming. Every decision, every challenge, every expectation suddenly seemed enormous. What if I made the wrong call? What if I couldn't earn the trust of the staff? What if I failed the students? What if I wasn't enough? The fear of failure became paralyzing at times, making me question whether I was truly capable.

God speaks into those moments of uncertainty, replacing the lies in our minds with His truth. In Judges 6:14, God tells Gideon, "Go in the strength that you have and save Israel out of Midian's hands. Am I not sending you?" Maybe you see yourself in Gideon right now—doubting your abilities, feeling unprepared, questioning whether you're the right person for the task ahead, at work or in your home. Gideon had already been told, "The Lord is with you," yet he still wrestled with doubt. Just as God reminded Gideon, He reminds us: Go in the strength that you have—and remember Who is sending you. As I transitioned into my new role, God helped me see that success wasn't about being the perfect principal. It was about obedience, faith, and trust in Him. I didn't have to rely on my own strength because God was with me. If you're feeling uncertain or overwhelmed today, take the next step in faith. Go in the strength that you have, knowing that God has sent you for such a time as this (Esther 4:14).

**Journal:** What areas of your life make you feel uncertain or unqualified? How would your perspective change if you truly believed that God has sent you and is with you?

**One-sentence prayer:** Heavenly Father, when doubt creeps in, help me to trust that You have called me, You are with me, and Your strength is enough for me.

*Further hope and encouragement: Gideon 6*

# DAY 164
# Get Dressed

*Finally, be strong in the Lord and in his mighty power. Put on the full armor of God, so that you can take your stand against the devil's schemes.*
*Ephesians 6:10*

It's time to prepare for the day ahead. When my kids were younger, Carly and I would help them get dressed each morning—a simple but powerful reminder that they couldn't do it on their own. My son would often call from his room, "Daddy, I need your help. I can't get dressed by myself!" But there were also days when he tried to dress himself. The problem? He was often unprepared for the conditions outside—wearing shorts on a freezing morning or bundling up in a sweatshirt when it was hot. Some days, his socks didn't match, or he was missing one altogether. He thought he was ready, but he wasn't dressed for what the day would bring.

How often do we do the same thing spiritually? We try to step into the day on our own, only to realize we're either wearing the wrong "clothes" or haven't gotten dressed at all—we're not equipped for the battles ahead. Maybe we face temptation without the belt of truth to keep us grounded or the breastplate of righteousness in place. Perhaps we encounter conflict but lack the gospel of peace to steady us. Or maybe we enter a difficult situation unprotected because we've left behind our shield of faith and helmet of salvation (v. 14-17). The truth is, when we try to "get dressed" on our own, we won't be prepared for the battles ahead. So, each morning as you get dressed, take a moment to clothe yourself with the full armor of God. Stay connected to Scripture—reading, listening, praying, and growing in your relationship with Him. That simple cry—"Father, I need Your help. I can't get dressed by myself!"—isn't just for children. It's a daily reminder for all of us. Today is significant. Be fully prepared. Don't step into the day spiritually unprepared.

**Journal:** In what areas of your life have you been trying to rely on your own strength? How can you better "put on the armor of God" in those areas today?

**One-sentence prayer:** Heavenly Father, help me to rely on Your strength today and clothe myself in Your full armor.

*Further hope and encouragement: Ephesians 6:10-18*

# DAY 165
# Busy Season

*"Martha, Martha," the Lord answered, "you are worried and upset about many things, but few things are needed—or indeed only one. Mary has chosen what is better, and it will not be taken away from her."*
*Luke 10:41-42*

I vividly remember the conversation with Carly. She gently pointed out that I hadn't been home much, that I was missing dinner with my family, and that when I was home, I wasn't myself—impatient and easily frustrated. Work had been overwhelming, and I assured her it was just a busy season, that things would slow down. She kindly responded, "Zac, it's always a busy season." She was right. I paused and reflected: for the past five and a half years, life had been a busy season, and something needed to change. But knowing something needs to change and actually doing something about it are two very different things.

Carey Nieuwhof (2021) says, "You tell yourself it's a busy season, but if your busy season has no ending, it's not a busy season—it's your life." How often do we live in a constant state of busyness, believing the lie that rest will come later? But later never comes. In Luke 10:41-42, Jesus lovingly tells Martha that she is worried and upset about many things but that only one thing is truly needed. While Martha was caught up in all that needed to be done, Mary had chosen to sit at Jesus' feet. She had chosen what was better. Life will always be full of responsibilities, deadlines, and demands, but we must be intentional about choosing what truly matters—choosing what is better. We can't do it all. And we weren't meant to. Each day, we have the opportunity to pause, to sit at the feet of Jesus, and to allow Him to realign our priorities. Busyness is not a badge of honor. May we learn to slow down, seek God first, and trust that He will guide us in stewarding our time well—at work, at home, and in all the places that truly matter.

**Journal:** What areas of your life have become a constant busy season? How can you intentionally shift your priorities to focus on what truly matters?

**One-sentence prayer:** Heavenly Father, help me to slow down, seek You first, and trust that You will guide me in using my time wisely for what truly matters.

***Further hope and encouragement: Luke 10:38-42***

# DAY 166
# Security

*When I felt secure, I said, "I will never be shaken."*
*Psalm 30:6*

A s I lay in the hospital bed, insecurity and a sense of being shaken overwhelmed me. Just days earlier, everything had been unfolding according to my plans—I was working, exercising, coaching, and celebrating the release of a new book. Life was going "well." But now, I could barely breathe. Every breath was a struggle, my chest tightening with pain radiating through my back and ribs. My breathing was rapid and shallow, and the wheezing reminded me that something was seriously wrong. Hooked up to oxygen, I cried out to God, through His grace, praising Him even in my weakness and insecurity. "Help me, God," I pleaded, "I know I can't even take a breath on my own." Strother (cited in Spurgeon) said, "We are never in greater danger than in the sunshine of prosperity. To be always indulged by God and never taste of trouble is rather a token of God's neglect than of His tender love."

In Psalm 30:6, the Psalmist reflects on a time when he felt secure and said, "I will never be shaken." But that false sense of security can quickly be shattered, just as it was in my own life. Too often, we move through life with a false sense of security in ourselves. We prefer comfort, ease, and our meticulously laid plans. For me, when life is going as planned, that is when I tend to take my eyes off my Heavenly Father. Thankfully, God's tender love humbles us and reminds us of His sovereignty. It's similar to walking a trail—everything is going well, you're enjoying the hike and the beautiful surroundings, and suddenly, you encounter a steep cliff and find yourself close to the edge. I don't know what cliff you've faced, are facing, or will face in the future. What I do know is that God is always working for the good of those who love Him (Romans 8:28). This doesn't mean you won't encounter heartache, sickness, pain, or tears. It means that God's mighty hand is with you, reaching out as you navigate life's steep cliffs. Reach out, grasp His outstretched hand, and hold on tight. He is with you and will never let you go. God is your true source of security.

**Journal:** Think about a time when your sense of security was shaken. How did God show up in that moment? How can you better rely on His strength rather than your own when life feels uncertain?

**One-sentence prayer:** Heavenly Father, thank You for being my true source of security.

*Further hope and encouragement: 1 Samuel 17, Psalm 30*

# DAY 167
# Don't Love You Any Less

*Endure hardship as discipline; God is treating you as sons.*
*For what son is not disciplined by his father?*
*Hebrews 12:7*

I've had to discipline my kids many times, and to be honest, it's one of my least favorite things to do. I'm always trying to grow in this area, learning how to discipline in a way that guides and grows rather than just corrects. I remember one Sunday morning clearly—Sunday mornings always seem to bring extra challenges. I often joke that Lionel Richie wasn't getting kids ready for church when he wrote *Easy Like Sunday Morning*. That morning, my young son was struggling with talking back, and we had to address it. As we worked through the discipline process, his eyes welled up with tears. Carly and I stayed right by his side, making sure he knew we were there for him. When it was over, I knelt beside him, looked him in the eyes, and said, "Daddy doesn't love you any less. This doesn't change how I feel about you." Before we moved on, I wrapped my arms around him in a hug and reminded him how much I love him and how much God loves him.

We fall short every day. We are human beings living in a broken, fallen world. But God doesn't desire our perfection—He desires our heart. Just as I assured my son that discipline didn't change my love for him, our Heavenly Father, through His grace, assures us of the same. Hebrews 12:11 reminds us, "No discipline seems pleasant at the time, but painful. Later on, however, it produces a harvest of righteousness and peace for those who have been trained by it." In Psalm 23, David declares, "Your rod and your staff, they comfort me" (v. 4). A shepherd's rod corrects and guides, while the staff rescues and reassures. God's discipline works the same way—leading us back when we wander and holding us close when we struggle. Here's the great news: when we fall short and need God's discipline, He wraps His arms around us and says, "I love you. Your Father doesn't love you any less." Why? Because of what Jesus did on the cross.

**Journal:** Reflect on a time when you experienced God's discipline. How did it shape your heart and bring you closer to Him?

**One-sentence prayer:** Heavenly Father, thank You for loving me enough to discipline me knowing that it comes from a place of love and leads me closer to You.

***Further hope and encouragement: Hebrews 12:4-11, Proverbs 3:11-12***

# DAY 168
# What do you Desire?

*Delight yourself in the Lord, and he will give you the desires of your heart.*
*Psalm 37:4*

As our family spent time in the Dominican Republic, a common question we asked the people we met was, "What are your dreams for your kids?" One man's answer for his four-year-old son deeply encouraged and convicted me. Through a translator, he said, "My greatest desire is for my son to know Jesus Christ." Wow. I could probably say that, but do I mean it with all my heart? While my prideful heart might say that first, in reality, I often desire that my children do well in school, excel in athletics, go to college, get married, and have successful careers. I desire good health for them. It's not that desiring these things is inherently wrong, but they should be a byproduct of our one true desire: to know Christ. When I reflect on it, many of my desires for my children are earthly.

We are called to desire God and God alone. My desire for myself should be to approach the foot of the cross every day. "Delight yourself in the Lord, and he will give you the desires of your heart" (Psalm 37:4). When our hearts are focused on God and our deepest desire is to know Him, He aligns our desires with His will. My greatest desire for my kids—and for those around me—should be that they know Jesus Christ. So let me ask you today: What's your greatest desire? What's the greatest desire you have for your kids? What's the greatest desire for the people within and around your sphere of influence? Much like this man from a poverty-stricken area, who had so little in earthly possessions, your greatest desire will shape how you approach each and every day. May our greatest desire be that we and those around us know Jesus Christ.

**Journal:** What are the desires you hold most dearly for yourself and your loved ones? How do those desires align with God's will for your life and the lives of those around you? Write about one way you can refocus your desires to be in line with God's purpose today.

**One-sentence prayer:** Heavenly Father, help me to delight in You above all else, and may my desires be shaped by Your will

***Further hope and encouragement: Psalm 37***

## DAY 169
# Be Compassionate

*Rejoice with those who rejoice; mourn with those who mourn.*
*Romans 12:15*

Carly and I have three amazing kids. But at their current ages—13, 10, and 8—they sure can fight a lot. Parenting is one of the hardest things I've ever done. The daily challenge of navigating relationships is constant, but I know God is shaping my heart through it. Eliot's 5th-grade travel basketball season was incredible—twelve wins, only two losses, and one of the top teams in the league. Unfortunately, they lost in the first round of the playoffs to a team they had previously beaten twice. Tears filled Eliot's eyes as the season ended, and we headed home. Normally, the back seat would be filled with bickering, but this time was different. Breaking the silence, Olivia spoke up: "You played awesome tonight, Eliot." A few minutes earlier, I had noticed Olivia holding back tears as she watched her sister walk off the court. And Isaac—the younger brother and usual instigator (like his dad)? He said nothing. Just silence. And it was beautiful.

That car ride reminded me of the power of empathy and compassion—meeting people right where they are. As Romans 12:15 says, "Rejoice with those who rejoice; mourn with those who mourn." Olivia and Isaac may not have realized it, but they were living this out. Sometimes, like Olivia, people need just a few words to remind them they're seen, valued, and not alone. Other times, like Isaac, no words are needed at all—just presence. He may not have been able to explain it, but in his own way, he felt Eliot's disappointment and carried it with her. Olivia did, too. They had watched her put in the work, give her best, and come up short. They didn't try to fix it or offer advice—just shared in her heartache. This may seem like a simple example, but let me ask you: Who needs a word of encouragement from you today? And who just needs to know you're standing beside them, feeling what they feel? Who do you need to celebrate with in their walk with God? Who do you need to mourn with? God calls us to walk alongside one another—in joy, in sorrow, and everything in between. Look for that person to walk beside today.

**Journal:** Reflect on a time when someone showed you compassion—whether through words or silent presence. How did it impact you, and how can you offer that same compassion to someone today?

**One-sentence prayer:** Heavenly Father, help me have the eyes and heart to rejoice with those who rejoice and mourn with those who mourn.

*Further hope and encouragement: Luke 10:25-37, Romans 12:9-21*

# DAY 170
# Next Play

*You will keep in perfect peace him whose mind*
*is steadfast, because he trusts in you.*
*Isaiah 26:3*

Playing sports taught me so much about life. Most importantly, it built lifelong relationships. One of those relationships is with my high school basketball coach, Tim Glackin. My goodness, he pushed us hard as basketball players, but he loved us even harder. Because we knew he cared about us as people, we worked hard for him and for one another. As I reflect on my high school basketball experience, two words stand out—words I can still hear Coach Glackin saying loudly: "Next play!" Whether we turned the ball over, missed a shot, made a great play, or a not-so-great one, he ingrained those words in our minds: "Next play." The beauty of basketball is that you can't dwell on a single play for too long. The game moves fast—it doesn't stop. You must be ready for what's next.

Life can feel a lot like basketball. It moves quickly, with some pushing and shoving along the way. Maybe you're in a season where you keep "turning the ball over," feeling like you can't stop messing up. Or maybe you're shooting your shot but missing every single time—no matter how hard you try, nothing seems to go in. It's possible you're in a season where things are going well. Either way, the same truth applies:

When you go to bed after a tough day—Next play.

When you wake up struggling from yesterday—Next play.

When you face a hard moment during the day—Next play.

When you have a great moment during the day—Next play.

Next play, next play, next play.

Never let yourself get too high or too low. Trust in God. Remain steadfast—firm and unwavering (Isaiah 26:3) in what He has called you to do and always be ready for the next play.

**Journal:** Where in your life do you need to embrace a "next play" mindset instead of dwelling on past mistakes or successes?

**One-sentence prayer:** Heavenly Father, help me to trust You in every moment, in every season, remaining steadfast and ready for whatever comes next.

***Further hope and encouragement: Isaiah 26***

## DAY 171
# It's All Working Out

*You intended to harm me, but God intended it for good to*
*accomplish what is now being done, the saving of many lives.*
Genesis 50:20

One of my favorite parts of speaking across the country is the conversations that happen afterward. I love when God uses a piece of my story to connect with someone, and they, in turn, share a piece of their story with me. After speaking in Richmond, Virginia, I noticed an older woman lingering in the corner. She seemed to be waiting. Finally, she approached me and asked, "Can I talk to you?" She began to pour out her heart, sharing her faith in Jesus but also opening up about her recent struggles. One thing she said stood out above the rest: "For years, I thought I wasn't the type of person for whom things worked out in life. But then my perspective changed. I realized that, through God's grace, even when it didn't feel like it, everything was working out perfectly."

That powerful interaction reminded me of the story of Joseph. After years of betrayal, false accusations, and imprisonment, he looked back and told his brothers, "You intended to harm me, but God intended it for good to accomplish what is now being done, the saving of many lives" (Genesis 50:20). Joseph's circumstances didn't change overnight, but God was working all along, weaving together something greater than he could have imagined. What mindset do you have today? Do you find yourself thinking, "I'm not the type of person for whom anything works out in life"? Look, I don't know your story, and I won't pretend to. But here's what I do know: If you are a child of God, things are unfolding exactly as He has planned for your life. Too often, we want God to change our circumstances instead of asking Him to change us through our circumstances. The quote often attributed to C.S. Lewis (n.d) sums it up perfectly:, "Don't pray to change God; pray that God would change you." Like the woman at the conference, trust that—even when things don't seem to be going as planned—through God's grace, everything is working out exactly as planned for your greatest good and His glory.

**Journal:** Think about a time when things in your life didn't seem to be working out. Looking back, can you see how God was using that situation for your growth or His greater plan? How can you shift your mindset today to trust His process?

**One-sentence prayer:** Heavenly Father, help me trust that even when things don't seem to be going as planned, You are working everything out for my good and Your glory.

*Further hope and encouragement: Genesis 50:15-21*

## DAY 172

# What's Stealing Your Time?

*Be very careful, then, how you live—not as unwise but as wise,
making the most of every opportunity, because the days are evil.*
*Ephesians 5:15-16*

As I awoke in the early morning hours, I turned over to check my watch on the nightstand. It read 1:58 A.M. I lay there for a few minutes, then reached over to check again. This time, it said 3:02 A.M. What? Where did that hour go? I was certain I hadn't fallen asleep. It could have only been a few minutes. Oh—Daylight Savings Time. It was time to move the clocks forward an hour. When I first woke up at 1:58 A.M., I was excited for the opportunity to catch the time jumping to 3:00 A.M.—much like a young kid trying to stay up on Christmas Eve to catch Santa sneaking into the living room to eat the cookies they left out. The next morning, our family struggled to get ready for church on time because a few of us had overslept due to the time change. My daughter Eliot joked, "How dare they take that hour from me? That hour is very special!"

Let me ask you this today: What's stealing your time? What's causing you to miss the opportunities right in front of you? Scripture tells us: "Be very careful, then, how you live—not as unwise but as wise, making the most of every opportunity, because the days are evil." (Ephesians 5:15-16). Paul isn't just telling us to manage time better; he's urging us to recognize the opportunity—the specific, God-given moments where something meaningful should happen. Think about the moments we miss because we don't recognize the opportunity before us. Maybe you've had the urge to call a friend or check in on a family member but decided to do it later—only to find out they really could have used that conversation. Perhaps God nudged you to encourage someone, but you hesitated, and the moment passed. Just like missing the clock jump from 2:00 to 3:00 A.M., we don't always realize when we allow time to slip away and an opportunity has come and gone—until it's too late. Time is a gift. Don't waste it—steward every opportunity well.

**Journal:** What specific opportunities has God placed in your life recently? Are there any you feel you've missed? How can you be more intentional about recognizing and acting on God-given moments?

**One-sentence prayer:** Heavenly Father, open my eyes to the opportunities You place before me and give me the wisdom to make the most of them.

*Further hope and encouragement: Ephesians 5:15-21, Galatians 6:10*

## DAY 173

# Going Back to Your Purpose

*Then the word of the Lord came to Samuel: "I am grieved
that I have made Saul king, because he has turned away
from me and has not carried out my instructions."
1 Samuel 15:10-11*

As I was writing my second book, *Leading with People*, a battle broke out in my mind. The book was filled with Scripture to guide leaders through the challenges of leadership, specifically in walking alongside people. But then I started thinking about how I could sell more copies. One way was to remove the Scripture entirely or limit it to a single chapter toward the end, where I would tie in the importance of faith. The main reason I considered this change was so that public school districts might be more inclined to purchase the book in bulk for their leadership teams. I wanted schools across the country to use it for staff book studies. But if I kept the Scripture and maintained my focus on faith in Jesus, that likely wouldn't happen.

One Sunday evening, I shared this thought with my brother-in-law, Mike. As an educator himself, he listened closely. Then he responded with a simple yet profound question: "What's your purpose in writing this book?" I paused, and he reminded me of a conversation we had previously. I had told him that my purpose as a writer was to encourage leaders in their personal walk with Jesus so that they, in turn, could walk alongside others in faith. As I got caught up in visions of book sales and expanded speaking opportunities, I had lost sight of that purpose. Thankfully, Mike gently pointed me back to it. Here's the thing: we often set out with a clear purpose but sometimes lose our way. Today, take a moment to go back to yours. Write it down on a piece of paper or in a notebook. Then reflect—are you truly living it out, or have you drifted? If needed, make the necessary adjustments, and go glorify God in all that you do.

**Journal:** Have you ever felt yourself turning away from the purpose God has given you? What distractions or desires pulled you in another direction, and how can you refocus on His calling today?

**One-sentence prayer:** Heavenly Father, help me to stay focused on Your purpose for my life, resisting the distractions of this world so that I may faithfully carry out Your will.

***Further hope and encouragement: 1 Samuel 15***

## DAY 174
# Show Restraint

*Do not wear yourself out to get rich, have the wisdom to show restraint.*
*Proverbs 23:4*

I try to do too much. That statement may even be an understatement. As I write today's devotion, I recall an evening recently when I had four events on my calendar. Four! After a full day of serving as a school principal, I had an evening school event, a local speaking engagement, a 5th-grade travel basketball practice to coach, and a meeting at church. Naturally, I wanted to attend them all. I helped get the evening school event started before heading to my speaking engagement. I missed basketball practice, but as I left the speaking event, I told Carly I was planning to stop by the church meeting to catch at least the second half. Her response? "If you go to that meeting, I'm going to come in there and pull you out by the ear."

I married an amazing woman, and she knows my limits—even when I can't see them. OK, I *do* see my limits, but I often ignore them. Carly knows me better than I know myself and has seen me operate at an unsustainable pace far too many times. She'll say, "Zac, I'm worried about you. You're going to crash soon." How about you? Do you surround yourself with people who speak truth into your life? Do they hold you accountable? Do they encourage you when you need it or offer honest insight you might not want to hear? Proverbs 23:4 tells us "to have the wisdom to show restraint." This is an area where I often struggle, frequently choosing the burnout path over the sustainable one, which leaves me operating exhausted. We must exercise restraint and recognize when our efforts are becoming excessive or misaligned with our values. And, just as importantly, we want to model that example for those around us. Show restraint today.

**Journal:** Where in your life do you struggle to show restraint? Who are the people you trust to hold you accountable, and how can you invite them to speak truth into your life?

**One-sentence prayer:** Heavenly Father, give me the wisdom to show restraint and the humility to listen to those You've placed in my life.

***Further hope and encouragement: James 1, Proverbs 23***

# DAY 175
# Seeing Clearly

*The eye is the lamp of the body. If your eyes are good,*
*your whole body will be full of light.*
*Matthew 6:22*

When I was a fourth grader at Quarryville Elementary, something happened: I couldn't read the words on the chalkboard. It wasn't that I couldn't read them; I couldn't see them. I became that student who, when Mrs. Balderston called on someone to read from the board, would suddenly need to use the bathroom. Why? Because I didn't want her to call on me and have everyone realize I couldn't see. I needed help but didn't want to ask. Then came the school eye exam. They called us down to the nurse's office, where we held a spoon over each eye and read letters from a screen. Guess what? I couldn't even read the giant "E"! They sent a note home, but my mom responded with her famous line that our family often laughs about: "It's probably just allergies."

Months later, I finally went to the eye doctor, and Dr. O'Brien confirmed it—I needed glasses or contacts. Since I was active, I chose contacts. The day I walked out of that office, I'll never forget—I could see. I had known something was wrong, but as I stepped outside and saw the details on people's faces, the blades of grass, the flowers, and the birds, I realized how much I had been missing. It wasn't that I couldn't see at all—I just hadn't realized how dull and blurry everything had become. Life is the same way. We don't always realize how much we can't see. The world distracts us from life as God intended. Maybe you know something is off but, like me in fourth grade, try to hide it. It's easy to let distractions dull what God has planned for us—for our good and His glory. But when our eyes are fixed on Jesus, the things of this world grow strangely dim—not the other way around. See clearly today.

**Journal:** Think about a time when you didn't realize how much you were missing until something changed your perspective. How might God be inviting you to see more clearly in your life right now?

**One-sentence prayer:** Heavenly Father, open my eyes to see life as You intend, so that I may focus on Your truth and not be distracted by the world.

***Further hope and encouragement: Matthew 6:19-24, Psalm 119:18***

# DAY 176
# Let the Game Come to You

*There is a time for everything, and a season for every activity under heaven.*
*Ecclesiastes 3:1*

I love basketball. I played my whole life, and in high school, I was a scorer. I felt the pressure to put points on the board for my team. Some games, I came out forcing shots that weren't there, trying to make something happen instead of letting the game develop. Coach Glackin, who called me "Z" (I guess the last two letters took too much energy), would call a timeout and say—sometimes gently, sometimes not—"Z! Let the game come to you." And when I did, the right shots opened up naturally. Through the flow of the game, opportunities came without forcing them. But other times, I was too passive, waiting instead of attacking. That's when Coach would pull me aside and say, "Z! You gotta go—it's time to attack the basket." In basketball terms, that meant I needed to step up, be aggressive, and start looking to score.

Coach Glackin knew me, our team, and what we needed to win. Just like in basketball, life has moments when we need to wait and moments when we need to act. As Ecclesiastes 3:1 says, "There is a time for everything, and a season for every activity under heaven." Sometimes we force things—career moves, relationships, financial security, restoration, our "calling"—when the timing isn't right. We try to force open doors that aren't meant for us yet. In those moments, we need to pause and remember: Let the game come to you. Trust that, in time, the right opportunities will present themselves. But maybe you're on the other side—too hesitant, waiting when it's time to move. There are doors right in front of you that you assume are locked, but all you have to do is turn the handle. You gotta go—it's time to attack the basket. God has already placed opportunities before you, but it's time to step forward in faith. Not sure which one you are? Turn to God. Pray that He opens the right doors and closes the wrong ones. Seek His timing, His wisdom, and His guidance. And trust this: He is working all things for your greatest good and His glory (Romans 8:28). So today, trust His timing—let the game come to you...or is it time to attack the basket?

**Journal:** Right now in your life, do you need to let the game come to you and trust God's timing, or is He calling you to attack the basket and step forward in faith? How can you seek His guidance in making that decision?

**One-sentence prayer:** Heavenly Father, give me wisdom to discern when to wait patiently for Your timing and when to step forward in faith, trusting that You are guiding my path.

*Further hope and encouragement: Ecclesiastes 3:1-8*

# DAY 177
# Just Me

*And from that time on Saul kept a jealous eye on David.*
*1 Samuel 18:9*

Part of my daily routine is morning cardio. After my devotions, I love getting in a good sweat to start my day. One of my favorite ways to do this is on our Peloton bike. When Carly and I first got the bike, we explored its many features and, as a competitive person, appreciated the ability to compete against others during the workout. On the screen, there are two tabs—one labeled "Overall" and another labeled "Here Now." The "Overall" tab shows how my performance compares to everyone who has ever taken that ride, while the "Here Now" tab displays how I rank against others riding at the same time. Some workouts I tend to repeat, whether because of the music or the challenge. One morning, I found myself laser-focused on climbing the "Here Now" leaderboard, determined to pass as many people as possible. As the ride progressed, I locked in on one particular rider who was keeping pace with me. I pushed harder, determined to beat them. By the end of the ride, I had won.

But as I caught my breath, something else caught my eye—a tab I had never noticed before, simply labeled "Just Me." When I tapped on it, I realized this section showed how my performance compared to my previous attempts at the same ride. And guess what? The last time I had done this workout, I performed much better. I had been so consumed with beating others that I lost sight of my own growth. Instead of pushing myself to my personal best, I settled for being a little better than those around me. This is the danger of comparison. God has given each of us unique talents and a purpose to maximize for His Kingdom. Like the Peloton ride, our eyes often get fixed on others and what they're doing. Saul did this with David—keeping a close eye on him instead of focusing on his own calling, which led to jealousy and distraction, losing sight of his own calling as king. So today, don't try to be just a little better than someone else. Tap into the "Just Me" mindset. Keep your eyes on the purpose God has for you, and give your best in what He's called you to do—for your greatest good and His greatest glory.

**Journal:** In what areas of your life have you been more focused on comparing yourself to others rather than growing into who God has called you to be? How can you shift your focus back to maximizing the gifts He has given you?

**One-sentence prayer:** Heavenly Father, help me keep my eyes on You and the purpose You have for my life

*Further hope and encouragement: 1 Samuel 18, Hebrews 12:1-2*

## DAY 178
# Never Too Far Gone

*Neither height nor depth, nor anything else in all creation, will be able to separate us from the love of God that is in Christ Jesus our Lord.*
*Romans 8:39*

I fully recognize that I write about eating a lot. Writing this 180-day devotional book has revealed that struggle of mine. But when I'm trying to eat better, trying to eat healthier, guess what happens when I have just a little bit of chocolate or dessert? I immediately fall into the mindset of, "Welp, I started down this road, I might as well keep going." Then, I eat more chocolate, more candy, more desserts. It really is a vicious cycle. To offer a more serious example, after speaking at an event, a man stopped me afterward and asked if he could have a few minutes of my time. "Of course," I replied. He began: "How can God still love me? Most days, I feel like I'm too far gone. And when I feel like I'm too far gone, I keep going further and further away." His eyes welled up with tears as he shared a small part of his story with me in the conference room of the hotel. "I've made so many mistakes in life. How can God still love me?"

Does that sound like you? Have you been there before? You feel like you're just too far gone, questioning how God could still love you. And like me with the chocolate, once you're in that mindset, it's easy to think, "I've already messed up, so why not keep going?" The lies begin to whisper: "You've gone too far now. You can't come back from this." And instead of running to Jesus, we hide. We run further away. But let me tell you this: No matter how many mistakes you've made or how many times you've felt like you've blown it, you are never too far gone. Romans 8:39 reminds us that nothing and no one can separate us from the love of Christ. Don't hide. Don't run away. Run to Jesus. Run to the Father. He's right there, waiting with arms wide open, ready to restore and heal. Your mistakes don't define you. What defines you is the love of God through Christ Jesus. No matter where you've been, no matter how far you feel you've strayed, you are never too far gone.

**Journal:** Think about a time when you felt "too far gone." What made you feel that way, and what thoughts or actions caused you to pull further away instead of running to Jesus? How can you remind yourself of God's unchanging love in those moments moving forward and run to Him?

**One-sentence prayer:** Heavenly Father, help me to remember that no matter how far I've gone, Your love is always greater and I can always run to You

***Further hope and encouragement: Romans 8:31-39***

## DAY 179
# Highs, Lows, and...Cows?

*As you do not know the path of the wind, or how the body is formed in a mother's*
*womb, so you cannot understand the work of God, the Maker of all things.*
*Ecclesiastes 11:5*

I've only ever been in one cow accident. You're probably thinking that's a typo and I meant to write car, but nope. I mean cow. One late February evening, my family was on the way to my daughter's indoor softball practice. It was dark and foggy, the kind of night where I could hardly see while driving. We were only minutes away when, out of nowhere, something massive appeared around the bend. I slammed on the brakes, but it was too late. Thud. Before I knew it, a gigantic cow was rolling across the hood of our small black SUV. Yes, a cow. It tumbled off the front, landed on its feet, and hobbled away into the fog like it had somewhere important to be. It all happened so fast that I jumped out of the car, trying to process what in the world had just occurred. Moments later, an Amish man came walking toward me like he was strolling along a beach and calmly said. "My heifer got out, and I can't find it." I glanced at our dented hood, then back at him. "Well," I replied, "I think I found it."

By the time we got home, the kids were fine—already sketching out the great cow collision of 2023 complete with a cow sprawled across the hood. Life is kind of like that drive—none of us really know what's waiting around the next bend. It might be a season of hardship, where things don't go as planned. It might be a time of joy and celebration, where everything seems to be falling into place. Or it might be a cow. In our family, we've adapted the classic *Highs, Lows, and Buffaloes* reflection game to include *cows*. Highs are the best parts, lows are the tough parts, and cows—the wild card moments—are the surprises you never saw coming. But here's what I *do* know: Whether you're experiencing highs, lows, or cows, God is sovereign over every moment. I don't know what you faced yesterday, what you're facing today, or what tomorrow will bring—but I *do* know that whatever it is, it's part of His perfect plan. Trust Him today.

**Journal:** Think about a time when life took an unexpected turn—your own *cow moment*. How did you see God's hand in it, even if it wasn't clear at the time?

**One-sentence prayer:** Heavenly Father, help me trust You not only in the highs and lows but also in the unexpected moments, knowing that You are always in control.

*Further hope and encouragement: Ecclesiastes 11, Psalm 93*

# DAY 180
# Don't Waste Your Life

*Be very careful then, how you live—not as unwise but as wise, making
the most of every opportunity, because the days are evil.*
*Ephesians 5:15-16*

I was on a short vacation with Carly in beautiful Mystic, Connecticut, when I came across a sign outside a store. The words on the sign couldn't have been more wrong. It read:

"Not every day is precious. Waste today, you deserve it."

Let me reframe that sign to encourage you in your life:

"Every day is precious—day by day, moment by moment—do not waste today. We deserve nothing; yet, in His grace, God grants us everything."

Now, I understand that last phrase—"we deserve nothing"—might sound harsh at first. But it's a powerful reminder that everything we have—our time, talents, and even the breath in our lungs—is a gift from God.

Time is precious, and time is short. Yet too often, we let it slip through our fingers. Scripture urges us to make the most of every opportunity because the days are fleeting and filled with distractions. Donald Whitney notes, "The more scarce something is, the more valuable it is." While most things we lose can be regained, time is not one of them. Once it's gone, it's gone. We are called to be good stewards of the time God has entrusted to us. That means using it intentionally—not just for productivity's sake, but for His glory. Stewarding our time well involves focusing on what truly matters: building relationships, growing in our faith, and living out our purpose. Don't wait until this life is nearly over to begin valuing your days. God has entrusted you with gifts—not for self-indulgence, but for your good and His glory. Each day is a divine opportunity to steward these gifts wisely. As you journey forward, remember that a life of purpose is built day by day—through faithful, intentional steps taken in the present moment. So, make the most of today. Embrace each moment with wisdom and gratitude. Live each day in light of eternity. Don't waste today. Don't waste your life.

**Journal:** Reflect on the journey you've taken through this devotional. How has focusing on living day by day deepened your relationship with God? What is one specific way you can continue to embrace each day with intention and purpose, trusting in His guidance?

**One-sentence prayer:** Heavenly Father, teach me to value each day You've given me and use it wisely for Your glory.

***Further hope and encouragement: Ephesians 5***

# Conclusion

As you close the final page of this 180-day journey, take a moment to reflect on the path you've walked. Each day has been an invitation to slow down, to draw near to God, and to let His Word shape your heart. These daily steps have not been about checking boxes but about cultivating a deeper relationship with the One who gives us life and purpose.

While this devotional may be ending, your journey is far from over. The habits of grace you've nurtured—immersing yourself in Scripture, engaging in heartfelt prayer, and walking in community—are not just practices for a season but rhythms for a lifetime. They are the means by which we continue to grow, to be transformed, and to reflect God's goodness in our everyday lives.

Remember, life is lived one day at a time. Each new day is an opportunity to experience God's mercies anew, to find strength in His presence, and to walk in the hope and encouragement that only He can provide. Let the truths you've encountered over these past 180 days continue to guide you, to anchor you, and to inspire you as you move forward.

So, take the next step, and the one after that, trusting that God is with you every moment. May your days be filled with the hope that comes from knowing Him and the encouragement that flows from walking in His ways—day by day.

# References

Botkin, K. (2020, April 18). *How Kobe Bryant forged such a strong relationship with Michael Jordan, according to their shared trainer.* CBS Sports. https://www.cbssports.com/nba/news/how-kobe-bryant-forged-such-a-strong-relationship-with-michael-jordan-according-to-their-shared-trainer/

Brooks, David. "*The Road to Character.*" The New York Times, 11 Apr. 2015, www.nytimes.com/2015/04/12/opinion/sunday/the-road-to-character.html.

Chapman, G. (2015). *The five love languages: The secret to love that lasts* (20th anniversary ed.). Northfield Publishing.

Drucker, P. F. (1967). *The effective executive.* Harper & Row.

Goff, B. (2018). *Everybody, always: Becoming love in a world full of setbacks and difficult people.* Thomas Nelson.

Manton, T. (2000). *A Puritan Golden Treasury* (I.D.E. Thomas, Ed.). Banner of Truth.

Mathis, D. (2016). *Habits of grace: Enjoying Jesus through the spiritual disciplines* (p. 88). Crossway.

Nieuwhof, C. (2021). *At your best: How to get time, energy, and priorities working in your favor.* WaterBrook.

Piper, J. (2020, March 18). *What to do if you wake up feeling fragile.* Desiring God.

Rohn, J. (n.d.). *Jim Rohn Quotes.* Jim Rohn International. Retrieved April 9, 2025, from https://www.jimrohn.com

Tozer, A. W. (1981). *This world: Playground or battleground?* Christian Publications.

Tripp, P. D. (2014). *New morning mercies: A daily gospel devotional*. Crossway.

Watson, T. (1981). *Puritan sermons* (Vol. 2, p. 62). Richard Owen Roberts.

Whitney, D. (2014). *Spiritual disciplines for the Christian life*. NavPress.

Zemeckis, Robert, director. *Forrest Gump*. Paramount Pictures, 1994.

# About the Author

Zac Bauermaster is an educational leader who is passionate about people. He currently serves as principal of Providence Elementary School, where he has the tremendous opportunity to lead teachers, support staff, families, and—most importantly—the next generation each day. His greatest joy in education is watching adults leverage their God-given talents to inspire kids to discover and use their own gifts. He is committed to creating an encouraging school environment where adults want to work, kids are excited to learn, and families trust and are proud to send their children.

In addition to his role as principal, Zac is a speaker and author. His first book, *Leading with a Humble Heart: A 40-Day Devotional for Leaders*, was released in July 2022. His second book, *Leading with People: A Six Pillar Framework for Fruitful Leadership*, followed in October 2023. Most recently, in 2024, Zac co-authored a children's book with his daughter Olivia titled *Lemon-Aid: Spreading Kindness One Cup at a Time*.

Zac is a husband to his best friend, Carly, and the proud father of three young children: Olivia, Eliot, and Isaac. He is a firm believer in leading his family first and is passionate about growing and encouraging leaders both in their workplaces and in their homes.

Most importantly, Zac loves Jesus, the Light of the world, and seeks to reflect and share that light with others in all he does. Learn more about Zac at www.zacbauermaster.com.

# More from ConnectEDD Publishing

Since 2015, ConnectEDD has worked to transform education by empowering educators to become better-equipped to teach, learn, and lead. What started as a small company designed to provide professional learning events for educators has grown to include a variety of services to help educators and administrators address essential challenges. ConnectEDD offers instructional and leadership coaching, professional development workshops focusing on a variety of educational topics, a roster of nationally recognized educator associates who possess hands-on knowledge and experience, educational conferences custom-designed to meet the specific needs of schools, districts, and state/national organizations, and ongoing, personalized support, both virtually and onsite. In 2020, ConnectEDD expanded to include publishing services designed to provide busy educators with books and resources consisting of practical information on a wide variety of teaching, learning, and leadership topics. Please visit us online at connecteddpublishing.com or contact us at: info@connecteddpublishing.com

## Recent Publications:

*Live Your Excellence: Action Guide* by Jimmy Casas

*Culturize: Action Guide* by Jimmy Casas

*Daily Inspiration for Educators: Positive Thoughts for Every Day of the Year* by Jimmy Casas

*Eyes on Culture: Multiply Excellence in Your School* by Emily Paschall

*Pause. Breathe. Flourish. Living Your Best Life as an Educator* by William D. Parker

*L.E.A.R.N.E.R. Finding the True, Good, and Beautiful in Education* by Marita Diffenbaugh

*Educator Reflection Tips Volume II: Refining Our Practice* by Jami Fowler-White

*Handle With Care: Managing Difficult Situations in Schools with Dignity and Respect* by Jimmy Casas and Joy Kelly

*Disruptive Thinking: Preparing Learners for Their Future* by Eric Sheninger

*Permission to be Great: Increasing Engagement in Your School* by Dan Butler

*Daily Inspiration for Educators: Positive Thoughts for Every Day of the Year, Volume II* by Jimmy Casas

*The 6 Literacy Levers: Creating a Community of Readers* by Brad Gustafson

*The Educator's ATLAS: Your Roadmap to Engagement* by Weston Kieschnick

*In This Season: Words for the Heart* by Todd Nesloney, LaNesha Tabb, Tanner Olson, and Alice Lee

*Leading with a Humble Heart: A 40-Day Devotional for Leaders* by Zac Bauermaster

*Recalibrate the Culture: Our Why...Our Work...Our Values* by Jimmy Casas

*Creating Curious Classrooms: The Beauty of Questions* by Emma Chiappetta

*Crafting the Culture: 45 Reflections on What Matters Most* by Joe Sanfelippo and Jeffrey Zoul

*Improving School Mental Health: The Thriving School Community Solution* by Charle Peck and Dr. Cameron Caswell

*Building Authenticity: A Blueprint for the Leader Inside You* by Todd Nesloney and Tyler Cook

*Connecting Through Conversation: A Playbook for Talking with Kids* by Erika Bare and Tiffany Burns

*The Dream Factory: Designing a Purposeful Life* by Mark Trumbo

*Stories Behind Stances: Creating Empathy Through Hearing "The Other Side"* by Chris Singleton

*Happy Eyes: Becoming All Things to All People* by Ryan Tillman

*The Generative Age: Artificial Intelligence and the Future of Education* by Alana Winnick

*Recalibrate the Culture: Action Guide* by Jimmy Casas

*Leading with PEOPLE: A Six Pillar Framework for Fruitful Leadership* by Zac Bauermaster

*A School Leader's Guide to Reclaiming Purpose* by Frederick C. Buskey

*Foundations of an Elite Culture: Building Success with High Standards and a Positive Environment* by David Arencibia

*Personalize: Meeting the Needs of All Learners* by Eric Sheninger and Nicki Slaugh

*The Five Principles of Educator Professionalism: Rebuilding Trust in Schools* by Nason Lollar

*Words on the Wall: Culturizing Your Classroom For Observable Impact* by Jimmy Casas and Cale Birk

*School of Engagement: 45 Activities to Ignite Student Learning* by Jonathan Alsheimer

*Intentional Instructional Moves: Strategic Steps to Accelerate Student Learning* by Sherry St. Clair

*Overcoming Education: Complex Challenges, Difficult People, and the Art of Making a Difference* by Brad R. Gustafson

*The Language of Behavior: A Framework to Elevate Student Success* by Charle Peck and Joshua Stamper

*Whose Permission Are You Waiting For? An Educator's Guide to Doing What You Love* by William D. Parker

*The Leader You're Not…And Why It's Just As Important As the Leader You Are* by Scott Borba

*The Growth-Minded Leader* by Tyler Cook

www.ingramcontent.com/pod-product-compliance
Lightning Source LLC
Chambersburg PA
CBHW060141130626
46556CB00006B/2447

* 9 7 9 8 9 9 9 8 8 3 6 1 5 2 *